The Value of Emily Dickinson

The Value of Emily Dickinson is the first compact introduction to Dickinson to focus primarily on her poems and why they have held, and continue to hold, such significance for readers. It addresses the question of literary value in light of current controversies dividing scholars, including those surrounding the critical issue of whether her writings are best appreciated as visual works of manuscript art or as rhymed and metered poems intended for the inner ear. Mary Loeffelholz deftly incorporates Dickinson's distinctive biography and her historical, religious, and cultural contexts into close readings, tracing the evolution of Dickinson's style. This volume – which considers not only the complex history of Dickinson's poems in print, but also their future in digital formats – will be an invaluable resource for undergraduate and graduate students seeking to better understand the importance of this seminal American poet.

Mary Loeffelholz is Professor of English and Vice Provost for Academic Affairs at Northeastern University. Her publications include *From School to Salon: Reading Nineteenth-Century American Women's Poetry; Experimental Lives: Women and Literature, 1900–1945;* and *Dickinson and the Boundaries of Feminist Theory.*

The Value of Emily Dickinson

Mary Loeffelholz
Northeastern University

CAMBRIDGE
UNIVERSITY PRESS

CAMBRIDGE
UNIVERSITY PRESS

University Printing House, Cambridge CB2 8BS, United Kingdom

One Liberty Plaza, 20th Floor, New York, NY 10006, USA

477 Williamstown Road, Port Melbourne, VIC 3207, Australia

4843/24, 2nd Floor, Ansari Road, Daryaganj, Delhi - 110002, India

79 Anson Road, #06-04/06, Singapore 079906

32 Avenue of the Americas, New York NY 10013-2473, USA

Cambridge University Press is part of the University of Cambridge.

It furthers the University's mission by disseminating knowledge in the pursuit of education, learning and research at the highest international levels of excellence.

www.cambridge.org
Information on this title: www.cambridge.org/9781107083912

First published 2016

A catalogue record for this publication is available from the British Library

Library of Congress Cataloging in Publication data
Loeffelholz, Mary, 1958–, author.
The value of Emily Dickinson / Mary Loeffelholz.
New York, NY : Cambridge University Press, 2016.
LCCN 2015040734 | ISBN 9781107083912 (hardback)
LCSH: Dickinson, Emily, 1830–1886 – Criticism and interpretation. | Dickinson, Emily, 1830–1886 – Appreciation. | Autobiography in literature. | Women poets, American – Biography. | Poets, American – 19th century – Biography. | Women and literature – United States – History – 19th century. | BISAC: LITERARY CRITICISM / Women Authors.
LCC PS1541.Z5 L5965 2016 | DDC 811/.4–dc23
LC record available at http://lccn.loc.gov/2015040734

ISBN 978-1-107-08391-2 Hardback

For Laura Morgan Green

The Mind lives on the Heart

Contents

Acknowledgments   *page* ix

Introduction   1
1   **The life of Dickinson's writing**   11
2   **Some striding – Giant – Love –**   37
3   **Women, now, queens, now!**   57
4   **Her American materials**   77
5   **Faith and doubt**   99
6   **The Spirit lasts – but in what mode –**   118

Notes   135
Bibliography   151
Index   159

Acknowledgments

For conceiving the *Value of* ... series and inviting me to contribute to it, I am deeply grateful to Ray Ryan and the Syndicate of the Cambridge University Press. For advice that improved this book, I thank Eliza Richards and two other anonymous readers for Cambridge. For reading its every word, and for so much more, this book is dedicated to Laura Green.

"A mutual plum is not a plum," wrote Emily Dickinson in reply to a friend who had addressed a letter jointly to her and her sister, Lavinia Dickinson: "I was too respectful to take the pulp, and do not like a stone. Send no union letters." The account of Emily Dickinson's value presented in this volume, however, is truly the mutual product of many more scholars than are individually cited in its pages. Against the grain of Dickinson's advice to "Send no union letters," I would like here to acknowledge the members of the Emily Dickinson International Society who have furthered my own work and that of many other Dickinson scholars since EDIS was chartered in 1988. Any errors in *The Value of Emily Dickinson* remain, of course, my own, as do the positions argued in matters of controversy among Dickinson scholars. I hope they will not stand in the way of readers' taking such fruit as they may find here, and leaving the stone.

Introduction
The value of Emily Dickinson

Emily Dickinson's writing remains valuable to a wide range of readers today. This I know because my first-generation Kindle™ tells me so; when it goes to sleep, its electronic ink every so often morphs into her image, surfacing in the screensaver's rotation of canonical authors along with the likenesses of Charlotte Brontë, James Joyce, John Milton, Sir Thomas More, John Steinbeck, Shakespeare, Mark Twain, and Virginia Woolf.

If I query my reading machine about what Dickinson is being valued *for*, though, matters become more complicated. The Dickinson presented to readers through the Kindle's screen has been retouched on multiple dimensions. The image's hyperfeminine lace ruff, curly hair, and heavy eyeliner are crude twentieth-century fabrications drawn onto the single indisputably authenticated daguerreotype likeness that remains of Dickinson, taken in 1847 – she was then just over sixteen years of age – now preserved in the Jones Library of Amherst College. A reader disconcerted by Dickinson's extreme Kindle makeover could strike back with the "Emily Dickinson Historic Vinyl Wall Graphic Decal Sticker," also available from Amazon.com – an imposing presence standing 60 inches tall, advertised as "Great for Parties."[1] Emily Dickinson as icebreaker? This unlikely version of Dickinson faithfully reproduces the flat hair and unadorned facial features of the famous daguerreotype, but alters Dickinson's dress to reveal her arms and neck: a wall sticker she may be but a wallflower she must not be, cost her image what it may in historical accuracy.

Less imposing but no less retouched are the Kindle store's most popular versions of Dickinson's writings: freely available digital transcriptions (made by volunteers in the Gutenberg Project) of the first, posthumously published volumes of Dickinson's poetry, edited by

Thomas Wentworth Higginson and Mabel Loomis Todd and now in the public domain. Like the Kindle screensaver image, the writings in *Poems of Emily Dickinson* (edited by Higginson and Todd, 1890), *Poems of Emily Dickinson, Second Series* (Higginson and Todd, 1891), and *Poems of Emily Dickinson, Third Series* (edited by Todd on her own, 1896) were altered for public circulation, well ahead of their later migration into digital format: their spelling and punctuation altered to conform to late nineteenth-century norms, their stanza forms regularized, they appeared under titles ("The Secret," "The Lonely House") and in thematic groups ("Life," "Love") never assigned them by Dickinson herself.

In making these alterations – in selecting from the bundles and stacks of manuscript writing left behind at her death what they saw as Dickinson's most finished and accessible verses; scraping away what they construed as minor errors of spelling, informal habits of punctuation, and happenstance line breaks dictated by the margins of her stationery; and thus separating the essence of the poems from the accidents of their transcription – Dickinson's early editors believed themselves to be enhancing the value of her work for contemporary readers. Even so, it was not long before they had second thoughts about the "very few and superficial" editorial changes they confessed to having introduced in the course of bringing Dickinson's work into print. In atonement, their *Second Series* of Dickinson's poems offered readers a facsimile of one of the surviving manuscripts of a poem published in the 1890 *Poems* as "Renunciation" ("There came a day – At Summer's full –"). Occupying four full pages ahead of the front matter of the slender volume, the facsimile and Todd's accompanying preface introduced Dickinson's rapidly growing print audience to aspects of her writing previously valued, if valued at all, only by her familiar correspondents: the increasingly "bolder and more abrupt" character of her handwriting's departure from "the delicate, running hand" expected "of our elder gentlewomen"; the generous spacing that set off words and even individual letters on the page; the rhythmic tic of her dashes; the hiatus of frequent visual line breaks inhibiting the forward momentum of familiar stanza forms.[2]

There would be more editorial controversy to come in the century following Higginson and Todd's first volumes, controversy that continues today even as Dickinson's work migrates into electronic formats vastly more sophisticated than the Gutenberg Project's austerely text-based, type-faced, nostalgia-provoking interface. To a remarkable degree, though, Higginson's and Todd's editorial dilemmas of the 1890s delineate fault lines along which present-day readers – and by no means only scholarly readers – continue to divide. More than scholarly completeness for its own sake is in question when editors debate how best to represent Dickinson's manuscript writings in print, in facsimile, or in digital images. No other poet of Dickinson's stature writing in English comes to us so completely through the efforts of posthumous editors (only Gerard Manley Hopkins comes close), and differing editorial presentations of Dickinson's writing embody different arguments for why Dickinson matters. Although I will not pursue editorial history for its own sake in this book, I will not avoid it where compelling and competing interpretations of Dickinson's value are tied to editorial decisions.

Do we value Dickinson's own distinctive punctuation? This would seem an easy question to begin with: few readers today would trade her original practices for more conventional usage, especially the dashes that set off words and slow the rhythm of lines, and with which Dickinson almost always ended her poems. But are the marks we refer to, for convenience, as Dickinson's dashes truly conventional dashes? Many readers have thought not. The editor of the first twentieth-century scholarly edition of her poems, Thomas H. Johnson, indicated them with the shorter en-dash, set off with spaces before and after, rather than the printer's conventional long, joined-up em-dash (like this "–", instead of like this "—"); Ralph W. Franklin's 1998 variorum edition prints them at hyphen length, thus producing on the printed page something still closer in appearance to the abbreviated marks of Dickinson's manuscripts. Has our experience of Dickinson's writing altered, if subliminally, with these changes? Other readers have gone further, locating expressive value even in the shape of Dickinson's letters and the variable spacing between words – as variable and as meaningful, argues poet Susan Howe, as when poets in our own day deliberately manipulate spaces within lines as well as between them. By the same logic, Howe objects strenuously to Franklin's editorial decision to print Dickinson's poems in regular stanza forms, arguing that the visual line breaks created by Dickinson's increasingly spacious handwriting are meaningful rather than accidental run-overs.[3] How much of Dickinson's value to us inheres in the creative freedom of her manuscript hand?

Do we value Dickinson's own word choices? Surely an easy question. The kind of gratuitous editorial interference exercised by Higginson and Todd in this respect – replacing Dickinson's "White Sustenance" with "pale sustenance," for example, in her great lament "I cannot live with you" (Fr 706) – is unimaginable today. The bridal and Eucharistic resonance of white that leaps from this poem to others such as "Mine – by the Right of the White Election" (Fr 411) and "Dare you see a Soul at the White Heat" (Fr 401), the contagion between "White Sustenance" and "Wild Nights" (Fr 269), and the image of her white dress preserved at her Amherst home are all part of Dickinson's value for us. But when she herself didn't choose among her words? The surviving manuscript of "I could not live with you" shows that Dickinson recorded two possible alternatives for "Sustenance": "exercise –" and "privilege –," as if to conjugate whiteness on an aesthetic and even political continuum running from bare bodily existence through self-willed, self-fashioning practice to aristocratic election. Many other of her poems survive with comparable alternative readings, most of them in the small, hand-stitched copybooks that Todd christened Dickinson's "fascicles." Todd also cut the fascicles' binding strings and dispersed their folded sheets for her own convenience in her editorial labors. Do the variants add to the value of "I cannot live with you"? Did Todd destroy something of literary value in scattering Dickinson's manuscript books?

Readers who value Dickinson's variants point to her manuscript books, painstakingly reconstructed by twentieth-century scholars, as evidence for Dickinson's practice of "choosing not choosing" (in the title of Sharon Cameron's influential study of the fascicles[4]) and argue that conventional print publication in her own day would have denied Dickinson the creative and cognitive freedom realized in her own book-making. Some value the fascicles as poetic sequences in which Dickinson's typically brief verses generate larger patterns of meaning: comparable to Whitman's sequences of the Civil War, perhaps related to the same national convulsion, and equally prescient, according to critics Rosenthal and Gall, as templates for the landmark lyric sequences of twentieth-century poetry by writers such as Pound, Williams, Yeats, Eliot, and Plath.[5]

Other readers prize aspects of Dickinson's writing that stray further still from the conventions of the printed volume of poems. Dickinson's "radical scatters" of the 1870s and 1880s, as Marta Werner calls them – her fragments, many of them penciled up, down, and aslant on scraps of stationery and wrapping paper – attract readers attuned to "the beauties of transition and isolation," contingency and discontinuity.[6] For Werner, the late fragments represent a fully autonomous aesthetic practice rather than tantalizing drafts of unrealized poems. Other readers nominate the intermingling of Dickinson's poetry with her letters – letters enclosing copies of poems; letters with inset poems; letters in which prose modulates directly into poems; letters composed wholly as poems, set off by little more than opening salutation and closing signature – as Dickinson's most characteristic and distinctive medium, not just a felicitous social recycling of poems composed for more autonomous aesthetic ends. More than 600 manuscripts of poems sent to correspondents in her lifetime survive, and how many more were sent we cannot know. Like the fascicles, the letters contest Robert Weisbuch's characterization of Dickinson's isolate poems as typically "sceneless" and shorn of occasion,[7] testifying instead to the work of the poem as gift, as flirtatious token, as intervention in grief and anger, as wordplay on the rose or lily, or pair of knitted garters, or even dead cricket sent along with it. For Virginia Jackson, what is most radical and significant about Dickinson's writing is precisely this direct address to a particular reader on a particular occasion. Challenging the "cultural consensus that Dickinson wrote poems," Jackson asserts that "lyric poetry as discourse immediately and intimately addressed to the reader precisely because it is not addressed to anyone at all" is exactly what

Dickinson did *not* write.[8] What Jackson values in Dickinson is, in a certain strong sense, unpublishable, even in facsimile reproduction, whether on paper or in pixels; it was never intended, she argues, for third-party eyes.

Martha Nell Smith also values the letters' personal address, but sees Dickinson's letters as her chosen mode of self-publication, "a consciously designed alternative mode of textual reproduction and distribution."[9] Whatever Dickinson's degree of participation or consent in the appearance of the very few poems printed during her own lifetime (eleven have surfaced to date), there can be no doubt of the energy and care with which she circulated her poems in correspondence any more than there can be doubt of the energy and care with which she recorded them in her manuscript books. In both modes, letters and fascicles, she did not have to see her poems tailored to the conventions of her surrounding print culture. The medium of correspondence mattered to her. How does it matter for Dickinson's value to us now?

This book will advance an argument for the value of attending to the life of Dickinson's writing, including the large contours of its material and compositional life: the emergence and fading of the fascicles, the ebb and flow of correspondences, the improvisational flair of the fragments. But the central units of value for my study will be poems more often than fascicles, fragments, or letters; and, most fundamentally, poems more often than their manuscripts. Along with her editor Ralph Franklin, I will hold that "a literary work is separable from its artifact, as Dickinson herself demonstrated as she moved her poems from one piece of paper to another."[10] Although Dickinson's wide-open handwriting and her short, broken lines are arresting in her later manuscripts, I will mostly follow Franklin in presenting the metrical stanza as more powerful than the visual line for organizing Dickinson's poems. I will be more concerned with those aspects of Dickinson's poems that handily survive translation into print or transcription by another hand – semantics and syntax, thematic clusters, meter and rhyme – than with aspects of her manuscript writings that are highly fragile or sensitive or altogether inaccessible to this translation.

Even as I was writing this book, however, the Houghton Library and Harvard University Press in October 2013 launched the Emily Dickinson Archive, the goal of which is "to make high-resolution images of manuscripts of Dickinson's poetry and letters available in open access, along with transcriptions and annotations from historical and scholarly editions" from Higginson and Todd forward. I serve on the advisory board of EDA, as the board members call it over email, and so presumably have some conviction of its value and its potential to "inspire new scholarship and discourse on this literary icon," in the words of our collective blurb for our work.[11] Harvard's adding its materials to the considerable collection of Dickinson manuscripts already online through Amherst College removes a significant barrier to widespread appreciation for the manuscript conditions of Dickinson's artistry, and readers around the world who will never be granted access to the originals (increasingly, most of us) will now find it much easier to make their own judgments about the significance of what gets lost in print translations of Dickinson's work. Why continue to make a point, then, of valuing poems over their manuscript artifacts, or metrical stanzas reconstructed by the inner ear over the visual line breaks conditioned by the size of the paper on which Dickinson copied her poems? Indeed, why continue to assume, *pace* Virginia Jackson's and other influential arguments to the contrary, that Dickinson wrote poems that can be extracted without essential violence from the original manuscript circumstances of their composition and circulation? In the age of high-speed Internet connections, why extract anything? Why not choose not choosing?

This book will return to these questions in its final chapter. Of course, EDA's launch has provided scholars as well as general readers with immensely easier access to the riches of the Dickinson archive. More eyes will bring more intelligence to questions of dating and the relationship of one manuscript to another, perhaps to find patterns that have not yet emerged to scholars. Decoding Dickinson's manuscript hand takes practice, so the electronic archive may give visitors who are not scholars a more vivid apprehension of what editors and scholars do – no bad thing at a time when this work is undervalued. There is historical value in providing readers as well with a more vivid apprehension of "the literate traces of [Dickinson's] everyday life," in Virginia Jackson's happy phrase,[12] and value in presenting wider opportunities to assess the various claims made on behalf of their literary importance. There will be little to regret and much to celebrate if my Kindle's frilly retouched image of Dickinson finally loses its hold on the public eye in favor of the high-resolution, meticulously curated manuscript images now widely available through the Emily Dickinson Archive.

But there will be less to celebrate, in my view, if the EDA's superb resources lend their weight to an image of Dickinson as intrinsically violated by the conditions of her translation from manuscript into print. To my mind, this image (no less than that doctored, virginal daguerreotype) plays to a gendered stereotype of woman's virtue and women's writing as something both material and fragile: a hymenal page that can only be damaged or destroyed in the processes of handling and circulation, inviting us to look but not touch or interpret. For all the genuine critical interest of Dickinson's compositional media, I believe that she too thought of a poem as exceeding its material artifact, in something of the way that "The Brain – is wider than the Sky –":

> For – put them side by side –
> The one the other will contain*   *include
> With ease – and You – beside –
> The Brain is deeper than the sea –
> For – hold them – Blue to Blue –
> The one the other will absorb –
> As sponges – Buckets – do –
> The Brain is just the weight of God –
> For – Heft them – Pound for Pound –
> And they will differ – if they do –
> As Syllable from Sound –   *(Fr 598A)*

The Brain is "wider" because human language and thought represent the material world at large; the sky and sea cannot reciprocate the brain's representational capacity, including its scandalous reflexive capacity – the object of Dickinson's play in this poem – to represent itself to itself. True, Dickinson here does not conceive of language and thought as existing in any way *apart from* their physical media: it is the spongy human brain, rather than a more abstract mind, that is weighed here and found sufficient (with a glimpse of the kitchen or the dissection table, or even the Civil War hospital[13]). Matter in all of its phases – liquid, solid, and gas (ink, page, and sounded syllable) – remains for Dickinson the condition of possibility for all human thought and language, underlined in this poem's metaphors and similes as they shuttle back and forth between material and immaterial containment, literal and metaphorical depth, sensation and abstraction, contrast and likeness.

According to this poem, however, the ultimate material substrate of Dickinson's poetry is not the manuscript page but rather the human brain itself, which mediates the architecture of sound and sense that unfolds between the reader's eye and her inner ear. To my eyes at least, the visual interest of the one surviving manuscript of this poem (bound into one of Dickinson's fascicles around 1863) pales next to the extravagant shocks delivered to all the senses through the poem's representational verbal art. Readers see and touch, perhaps even smell, this brain, all in words that resound to the inner ear. Highly regular as to meter and rhyme by Dickinson's standards, "The Brain – is wider than the Sky –" relies on alliteration, assonance, and repetition to underscore likeness and difference. The Brain and the sea in the second stanza initially share no overlapping sounds; but the alliteration linking "Brain" to "blue" to "Buckets" enacts in sound what the stanza asserts thematically: the brain absorbs the sea. Whether looking at a reproduction of Dickinson's own manuscript or a translation of her writing into conventional print, the reader who reconstitutes from the material traces of the written page the speech stream of sounded language can appreciate this poem's embodied play between the back-mouth, absorbent vowels and consonants of "sponges" and the plosive front-mouth consonants of "Buckets" as Dickinson demonstrates that articulate speech is both flowing and stopped, both liquid and contained.

It is, above all, close and careful reading of the poem as a sounded verbal artifact, more so than visual inspection of the poem's shape on the manuscript page, that unfolds the complexity of Dickinson's simultaneous allegiance to sensory experience and signifying abstraction. That complexity, I believe, is why we continue to value her writing. In Dickinson's representation, the human brain that mediates this act of reading is a remarkably robust organ, by contrast with the fragile materiality of the manuscript page: powerful, hefty, absorbent, equal to taking in the entire world. "The Brain – is wider than the Sky –" intimates that Dickinson's art works by absorbing and transforming its historical and cultural contexts (including the nineteenth century's growing scientific interest in the relationship between the mind and the brain); following this poem's lead, this book will draw on historical, cultural, and biographical contexts where they seem interpretively useful. Unlike the unique physical manuscript of a poem – which might have been sent to just one person, or, as in the case of this poem, was retained unshared by Dickinson during her lifetime – Dickinson's address in this poem to a generic "You" implies that the reproducible, intelligible forms of language are a shared cultural property; following this poem's lead, I will take note of where Dickinson addresses a poem or letter to an individual recipient, and will note as well where there is no surviving evidence of her having done so. In either case, the reproducible forms of syllable and sound – the poem investing its various material incarnations, the poem as transmitted from brain to brain to brain, the poem as object of close reading – will be the primary focus of this book.

Unless otherwise noted, Dickinson's poems are cited from R. W. Franklin's variorum edition of *The Poems of Emily Dickinson* (1998), by first line and the number assigned them in Franklin's chronology, and her letters from Thomas H. Johnson and Theodora Ward's edition of *The Letters of Emily Dickinson* (1958), by the number assigned to them in that edition. Unlike Franklin, however, I observe Dickinson's punctuation and capitalization in citing poems by first lines.

I The life of Dickinson's writing

In *The Life of the Poet* (1981), Lawrence Lipking proposes that "the image of a fulfilled poetic destiny – the life of the poet – continues to lure both poet and reader." The value of individual poems to both poets and readers, he argues, stems in part from their relationship to "the cumulative purpose – the career or destiny – that unites them."[1] The high value that readers set on the life of the poet reflects our own human investments in "self-making," as Edward Said calls it, which is not a prerogative reserved for poets alone; "all of us, by virtue of the simple fact of being conscious, are involved in constantly thinking about and making something of our lives."[2] The beginnings of poetic careers, according to Helen Vendler, echo and find artistic shape for the early stages of our common human self-making: "To the young writer, the search for a style is inexpressibly urgent; it parallels, on the aesthetic plane, the individual's psychological search for identity – that is, for an authentic self-hood and a fitting means for its unfolding."[3] Poets come into their own, as Lipking observes, in the process of learning to re-read and re-write their own earlier work, "in constant recoil from [their] earlier themes."[4] The "last great problematic" of artistic careers, Said proposes, is that of human life at large – "the last or late period of life, the decay of the body, the onset of ill health" – in response to which some artists take on, "near the end of their lives ... a new idiom, what I shall be calling a late style"; great instances of late style may register "the artist's mature subjectivity, stripped of hubris and pomposity, unashamed either of its fallibility or of the modest assurance it has gained as a result of age and exile."[5]

For much of the twentieth century, and by many critical readers, Emily Dickinson's writing was thought not to have a life, in Lipking's strong sense of "a fulfilled poetic destiny" accomplished over time.

What took its place were variations on "the Myth" of Amherst – in the phrase that village gossip began to use about Dickinson during her lifetime: the story of a woman who garbed herself in white, retreated to her father's house, and churned out hundreds of similar poems in the wake of a mysterious romantic rejection. The past three decades, however, have seen widespread rejection of David Porter's once uncontroversial assertion that Dickinson's "art did not change over more than two decades of composition."[6] Speaking for an emergent consensus, Dickinson biographer Alfred Habegger tartly observes that "With almost anyone else – Charles Dickens or George Eliot or Henry James or James Joyce or T. S. Eliot – it is taken for granted that the life has some shape or curve," and yet Dickinson's writings, across her life span, are treated as interchangeable chips off a uniform block: "It is as if this writer were freakishly unable to learn from experience, and wrote without traction all her life." Not so, Habegger believes: "The question of development is fundamental" to understanding Dickinson's poetry.[7] Although Habegger makes his claim for Dickinson's evolution from a comparative and biographical perspective focused on Dickinson's life as a sentient social being, readers compelled by the archive of Dickinson's manuscripts have come to similar conclusions, going as far back as Mabel Loomis Todd, who observed that as Dickinson "advanced in breadth of thought" her handwriting "grew bolder and more abrupt, until in her latest years each letter stood distinct and separate from its fellows."[8]

If the evidence for Dickinson's poetic development is so bold, though, how did the idea of her changelessness ever gain traction with readers? Habegger concedes that "it is true and indeed notorious that Dickinson wrote in the same few verse forms all her life, and that she always sounds like Dickinson, and that readers are easily lulled."[9] By way of example, the following two poems share a governing metaphor and a verse form (common meter, Dickinson's favorite: composed in iambic feet – a weak followed by a strong stress – with quatrains alternating lines of four feet and three feet, rhymed *abcb*) that is identical but for the dropped syllable in the final foot of three lines of exhibit A. Both poems start with the same syntactical structure: an adverbial phrase of *when* or *where*. Reader – are you lulled?

(A) When Roses cease to bloom, Sir,
And Violets are done –
When Bumblebees in solemn flight
Have passed beyond the Sun –
The hand that paused to gather
Opon this Summer's day
Will idle lie – in Auburn -
Then take my flowers – pray!

By permission of Amherst College Archives and Special Collections

(B) Where Roses would not dare to go,
     would risk
What Heart ~~could find~~ the way,
And so I send my Crimson Scouts
    sound
To ~~test~~ the Enemy –

A reader comparing these two poems in their manuscript forms will immediately see many of the gross differences between Dickinson's early and late manuscripts remarked on by Mabel Loomis Todd.

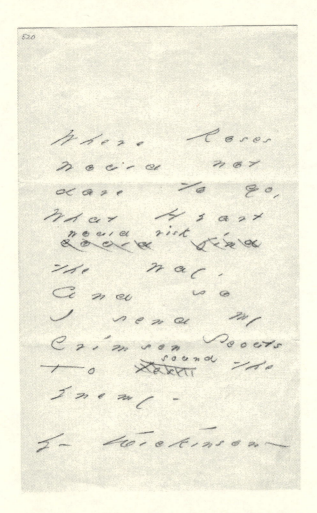

By permission of Amherst College Archives and Special Collections

"When Roses cease to bloom" is carefully copied out in pen, in a neat, right-slanting italic script, with no cancellations; the end of each metrical line coincides exactly with the end of each visual line. It shares its manuscript sheet with several other poems that Dickinson copied out together at the same time. By contrast, "Where Roses would not dare to go" is written in pencil and bears Dickinson's revisions. The handwriting of this manuscript poem is essentially print, the ligatures (connections between letters) absent, although the swooping capital "S" and "R" letters retain some likeness to those in "When Roses cease to bloom." The space between letters and words in "Where Roses would not dare to go" is so generous that the visual lines of the manuscript are only two or three words long; on the page, this poem occupies ten visual lines, as against its metrical form of four lines. These visible differences, among others, in the surviving manuscripts of the two poems help Dickinson's editor Ralph Franklin to date "When Roses cease to bloom" (Fr 8A) to 1858, near the beginning of Dickinson's most active years as a poet, and "Where Roses would not dare to go" (Fr 1610A) to 1883, just three years before Dickinson's death.

Allowing that Dickinson's manuscripts visibly evolve and change over her lifetime, what about the poems themselves as verbal artifacts? With or without the compelling visual evidence of changes in Dickinson's manuscript hand, I believe that "Where Roses would not dare to go," by contrast with "When Roses cease to bloom," is recognizably a song of experience, one that returns to the aesthetic values and problems of Dickinson's earliest poems in order to transform them.

"When Roses cease to bloom" positions its deliberately conventional dramatic characters – an unspecified "Sir," a flower-gathering woman – to make a conventional implicit claim on behalf of poetry: its flowers will endure while earthly flowers, as well as those who gather them, fade away. The poem's two quatrains face one another in a tidy chiasmus: dying flowers / living speaker // dead speaker / living flowers (of poetry), a closed rhetorical form set off by the perfect one-syllable rhymes of done / Sun, day / pray. The social distance of age, gender, or station in life implied between the speaker and "Sir" in the poem's first quatrain, and underscored metrically by the dropped foot's pause before "Sir," is posited as so great that only death can overcome it. Pity for the speaker's own anticipated death may (she ventures) move "Sir" to accept her proffered gift, the poetic flowers that will outlive her: "Then take my flowers"– *then* as in "at that later time, after my death," but also *then* as in "so" or "therefore." If the hand that gathered these flowers is mortal, however, so too will be the hand that may accept them: the small sting of this early poem lies in the contagion of human mortality, passed from hand to hand along with the speaker's undying flowers. The thematic import of "When Roses cease to bloom" aligns not only with its rhetorical structure and rhyme scheme, but also with the manuscript embodiment in which it comes down to us. Transcribed in ink, in a final version without corrections or additions, set down neatly, and marked off from other poems copied onto the same folded manuscript sheet, this poem along with other poems similarly copied around the summer of 1858 was then stitched into a small booklet of poems, which Dickinson retained: one of her earliest fascicles, probably the very first. She was beginning to gather her manuscript "flowers" into a form of some permanence.

Some twenty-five years later, "Where Roses would not dare to go" – written in pencil, cross-hatched with revisions, and signed "E. Dickinson" as if intended for sending as a letter – makes no claims at all for the immortality of poetry. Where the earlier poem depends on the implicit substitution of immortal poetic flowers for fading natural roses, the later quatrain lives for the here and now in which Dickinson's red roses, along with her poem, make a cautious approach toward enemy lines – presumably those of an estranged friend. The distance between Dickinson and her Enemy in this poem is not the mannered social distance separating the speaker from "Sir" in "When Roses cease to bloom"; it is a no-man's-land separating rival armies, a landscape recollected from the American Civil War. The beseeching girl of the earlier poem has become a wary field commander facing an equal adversary. Her "Crimson Scouts," Dickinson's epithet suggests – roses and words alike – can both wound and be wounded; neither immortal nor invincible, they serve her only with stealth, intelligence, and courage. The off-rhyme with which the quatrain ends – "way / Enemy" – underscores the poem's uncertain resolution: Dickinson does not know how her words will be received. The only word of more than two syllables in "Where Roses would not dare to go," "Enemy" ends the poem on a subordinate accented syllable, unsettling Dickinson's otherwise evenly stressed iambs. The poem's measured footfall strays over an invisible boundary in this final line; the Enemy has indeed been *sounded*.

Perhaps Dickinson's uncertainty about the poem's reception led her not to send it, or perhaps she judged her revisions extensive enough to call for transcribing a clean copy for the intended recipient. If she did re-copy and send the poem, that version (along with the recipient's identity) is lost to history. What we do know is that Dickinson preserved the surviving manuscript of "Where Roses would not dare to go" in its liminal condition: signed but unaddressed, anchored at one end to the biographical occasion of familiar correspondence but retained as a more autonomous aesthetic object. Here, as in the instance of "When Roses cease to bloom," the manuscript condition of the poem seems consonant with the kinds of aesthetic value embodied by the poem, considered as a verbal artifact of Dickinson's late style. "Where Roses would not dare to go" aligns poetry less with permanence or artistic resolution than with power, one of Dickinson's favorite words in her late writings: "Power is a familiar growth," begins another late poem (Fr 1287, circa 1873). In "Where Roses would not dare to go," poetry commands a formal language fully equal and open to the ambivalence of human intimacy, the aggression latent in any gift, and the spaces between human beings.

The remarkable differences between these two small poems, early and late – or, more accurately, their differences-within-similarities – point to the value of reading Dickinson's writings in light of what Habegger calls "some shape or curve" of development; the value, in other words, of a life of Dickinson's writing. Although dating her writings will never be without controversy, although we cannot know how many were destroyed, and although some biographical questions may never be solved, evidence for broad patterns and generic shifts – such as the beginning and end of the fascicles – survives in plenty and tells a story of quite fundamental evolution, over time, in Dickinson's vocation as a poet.

Both the hundreds of remarkable individual poems copied out during the years in which Dickinson assembled her fascicles (roughly 1858–1866) and the making of the fascicles themselves testify to Dickinson's high ambitions for her poetry of this period. Cristanne Miller observes that the poems of the fascicle years tend to be both longer and more metrically varied than Dickinson's later work;[10] thematically, they are also more occupied with matters of immortality and recognition and venture more explicit statements about poetry as craft and as vocation. How the fascicles began and how they changed during these peak years of Dickinson's poetic production is much easier to describe than why Dickinson, after the mid-1860s, ceased to create them. Scholars have speculated that difficulties with her eyesight, difficulties with the Dickinson household servants or lack of them, or some lapse of personal as well as national galvanizing purpose with the end of the Civil War contributed to Dickinson's abandonment of the fascicles as a means of organizing her work.[11] After the fascicles cease, Dickinson's poems become more occasional, more imbricated in the materials of daily life, less systematically preserved and self-curated. Scribbled on fragments of envelopes and on the reverse of advertisements, sent as notes to Susan Dickinson next door as well as to more distant friends, they deploy Dickinson's power over the incidents and relationships of ordinary life as if casually: "As casual as Rain / And as benign –," in the words of one late poem ("The Gentian has a parched Corolla –," Fr 1458, circa 1877). Toward the end of her life, Franklin observes, she "grew indifferent to making even second copies, with a number of poems surviving in their initial draft, laid down in a large running script"[12] – among them, "Where Roses would not dare to go." Dickinson's "indifferent" mode of composing, collecting, and circulating her late poems has something in common with what Erik Gray calls "the poetry of indifference" in British Romantic and Victorian poetry: less reaching after recognition, less concerned with aesthetic immortality, Dickinson's late work stands deliberately aside from "the claims that poetry usually makes for its own importance."[13]

This hasn't stopped readers – especially present-day readers – from making strong, even peremptory claims for the distinctive value of Dickinson's late writings. Many of the controversies now dividing scholars of Dickinson's poetry stem from the relative value placed by readers on Dickinson's early poetry versus her later, more dispersed work. Those who admire the self-organizing ambitions of Dickinson's fascicle poems tend to regard the quality of Dickinson's poems as having ebbed along with their quantity after the mid-1860s: Habegger, for example, dismisses her writing of the 1870s as a "large accumulation of drafts penciled on scraps of stationery, notepaper, or wrapping papers," mostly "a quantity of inferior work, some of it sketchy, repetitive, obscure."[14] The very same qualities, however, have lately drawn increasing numbers of readers to the manuscripts of Dickinson's later poems. To these readers, what appears as a humble occasional quatrain or an abandoned draft on the printed page looks more like experimental visual art when viewed in manuscript form, where Dickinson may inscribe her bold late handwriting across an advertisement or slant it into the angles of a torn envelope, as she did in one surviving version of "The Mushroom is the Elf of Plants" (Fr 1350B, circa 1874).

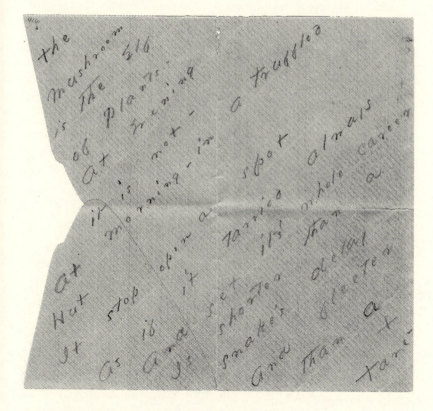

By permission of Amherst College Archives and Special Collections.

"Gorgeous nothings," their editors Jen Bervin and Marta Warner call these late writings, taking the phrase from an unclassifiable Dickinson fragment (not long enough to be characterized as poetry or prose, poem or letter) that survives at Amherst College.[15] To Werner's eyes, the startling originality of Dickinson's late works, obscured in standard print transcriptions, emerges when they are exhibited in their manuscript originals, published in full-color facsimile or presented online in high-resolution digital surrogates. In her late manuscripts, Werner believes, Dickinson's "calligraphy itself becomes expressive or aesthetic," unmoored from lexical meaning as it "responds unconsciously to the chance ordering of words across the page." Having reached, in these fragments, "the torn and asymmetrical edge" at which writing "passes over ... into risk or scattering," Dickinson's graphic medium becomes its own message, and "no gloss is possible."[16]

Dickinson's late writings matter and should continue to matter to readers; but not, I think, chiefly for their value as a visual art form. Countering Werner's premise that Dickinson envisioned her work as "primarily a visual phenomenon," Holland Cotter argues that, "conveyed in whatever medium, words are the fundamental matter of her art, what it is about, and what Dickinson was about." What matters most about the fragments of paper on which she composed many of her late poems, Cotter observes, is not their unglossable visual shapes but the layered meanings (including verbal meanings) they must already have borne for Dickinson: "Her chosen paper already carried words, familiar names and addresses. It was stained with life, with postmarked dates and the dust of distant places. From that resonant content, she could generate new content, just as she had always generated poetry from the immediate facts of the physical world." The "shock" of Dickinson's work comes, as Cotter asserts, "in the words, with other, lingering aftershocks following in the visual details of their settings."[17]

Cotter is right, both on the aesthetic merits and on the archival evidence. Striking as its inscription inside a torn envelope may be, the more important and lasting shock of a late poem such as "The Mushroom is the Elf of Plants" is that Dickinson wrote a poem about mushrooms (along with poems about rats, snakes, flies, and worms). This poem comes down to us in five surviving manuscripts and one transcript made from a copy that Dickinson sent to her cousins Louise and Frances Norcross; as a reader may ascertain from clicking through the versions collected online in the *Emily Dickinson Archive*, four of the five manuscripts are copied more or less conventionally, on conventional stationery. Given the number and character of the surviving manuscripts, it seems impossible to believe that their shared lexical content is reducible to an unconscious, spontaneous response to the glancing visual inspiration of a torn envelope.[18] What is significant about the manuscripts of "The Mushroom is the Elf of Plants" when considered as a group is not their visual forms, but rather their sheer number, the many revisions Dickinson recorded on them, and the fact that Dickinson sent the poem, in whole or in part, to her Norcross cousins and to Thomas Wentworth Higginson. The manuscript record suggests that Dickinson valued this poem, that she thought it might be accessible and interesting to her own contemporaries (she was right: Higginson and Todd included the version sent to the Norcross cousins in their second, 1891 volume of her poems), and that there was something she was trying to sharpen about its verbal art, not just its visual inscription.

Glossing the former rather than the latter, I suspect that Dickinson intended "The Mushroom is the Elf of Plants" as a self-consciously late *ars poetica*, yet one more reworking – like "Where Roses would not dare to go" – of her early pleas to "take my flowers – Pray!" Here is the poem in what is probably the last version Dickinson transcribed, around summer 1874:

The Mushroom is the Elf of Plants –
At Evening, it is not
At Morning, in a Truffled Hut
It stop opon a Spot

As if it tarried always
And yet it's whole Career

Is shorter than a Snake's Delay –
And fleeter than a Tare –

'Tis Vegetation's Juggler –
The Germ of Alibi –
Doth like a Bubble antedate
And like a Bubble, hie –

I feel as if the Grass was pleased
To have it intermit –
This surreptitious Scion
Of Summer's circumspect.

Had Nature any supple Face
Or could she one contemn –
Had Nature an Apostate –
That Mushroom – it is Him!   (*Fr 1350F*)

Like Yeats's great poem of his late career, "The Circus Animals' Desertion," "The Mushroom is the Elf of Plants" is a poem of desublimation.[19] Where the roses and violets of Dickinson's earliest poems are ideally beautiful and sadly perishable messengers, the mushroom is ugly, ephemeral, and deceptive; a wandering, hard-to-eradicate blemish on the otherwise smooth face of the lawn; the scion of a rogue Borgesian phylum that also encompasses snakes, weeds, and bubbles. Biologically not a plant at all, the mushroom as traveling confidence man or trickster feeds on vegetation's death and decay. The mushroom's role in recycling organic matter may be echoed in the phonemic economy of the poem's fourth line, which turns over and over its few elemental Germanic particles: *stop / opon / spot*. The same elemental phonemic particles return in the penultimate line of the poem, but there upcycled into Nature's melodramatic, Latinate accusation of the mushroom as her "Apostate," as if to imply that Nature and human language, and poets too, inevitably recirculate their materials – not just the used paper and envelopes that Dickinson reached for so often during the 1870s and 1880s, but also their primary verbal and figural elements. Just beyond the first stanza's insistent elemental rhymes of not / stop / upon / spot lies the poem's unspoken grounding in *rot*. (It lurks as well in Dickinson's variant for "Apostate" – "Iscariot" – in several of the manuscripts.) Extending her mushroom to Higginson and to Louise and Frances Norcross in 1874, Dickinson signaled her readiness to lay her flowers down in the decay from which all flowers start.

Dickinson's late work returns over and over again to its origins – a pattern of thinking and writing that many readers find moving and valuable, but also one reason why some of her readers see little change in her poems over time. How, then, did Dickinson begin? Recalling Helen Vendler's observation that a young poet's "search for a style is inexpressibly urgent" and linked to her search "for an authentic selfhood and a fitting means for its unfolding," it is striking how much of that early search for a style is hidden from us in Dickinson's case, apparently by her own design. Nothing of the verse she must have written as a schoolgirl has been uncovered. Two humorous poems survive from 1850 and 1852, but not from copies kept in Dickinson's possession (one was kept by a correspondent, another copied into a cousin's commonplace book and also published in the local *Springfield Daily Republican*). The earliest poem preserved in Dickinson's own records, "On this wondrous sea," was incorporated into a letter sent to Susan Dickinson in March 1853, and would be copied out again, around 1858, for Dickinson's first fascicle. Dickinson's letters to Henry Vaughn Emmons, an Amherst College student whom she befriended, suggest that by 1853 she was regularly sharing her poems with him and others in her circle, not just individually but also in groups – reciprocating his "beautiful writing" with "a few of my flowers," lending him a "little manuscript" on another occasion, and telling him of her intention to send "garlands" of poems to other friends (*Letters* 119, 121, 151). Almost no poems survive in Dickinson's own hand from these years, however – only the two included in letters to Susan. Ralph Franklin's hypothesis about the gap in the manuscript record seems inescapable: "There may have been a major stocktaking in 1858, a sifting and winnowing of her entire corpus – if there had not already been a destruction of manuscripts in the silent years preceding."[20]

Dickinson launched her fascicles, it seems, on a basis of selective destruction, rejecting at least in part her earlier poetic selfhood and the means by which she had so far "unfolded" it, in album and newspaper verse and in familiar correspondence.

> By such and such an offering
> To Mr So and So –
> The web of life is woven –
> So martyrs albums show!   (*Fr 47A, Fascicle 2, circa late 1858*)

What kind of book other than the album could she envision making, and who, if not "Mr So and So," would be its implied reader? Dickinson's earliest manuscript books of 1858–1859 struggle with the all-too-available model of the young lady's album along with the album's conventional organizing metaphor of the floral "offering" of poems; they alternate between testing the potential of this metaphor for a more rigorous kind of poetry and exploring other metaphors around which to organize her self-dedication to the work of writing. Each strand of metaphor tested in the earliest fascicles responds in its turn to a common set of questions: How far from my social origins, how far from the readily available conventions must I move in order to begin in an authentic way? How important will the recognition of others remain to me as I move? Can a poetic vocation even exist without legibility to others, outside of the common "web of life," apart from the possibility of poetic (and emotional and erotic) exchange?

In Fascicle 1, Dickinson marshals at least three organizing metaphors in response to these questions: the floral metaphor, metaphors of coinage connected to loss and recompense, and the metaphor of a voyaging boat.[21] Both "On this wondrous sea" (Fr 3) and "Adrift! A little boat adrift!" (Fr 6) start from the stock metaphor of the voyage of human life toward eternity. In its conventional form the metaphor asserts that, by whatever paths, human souls travel to the same ultimate destination; however eventful, movement away from one's origins is always movement toward a known end. When she sent "On this wondrous sea" to Susan Dickinson in 1853, Dickinson gave this conventional form of the metaphor a vocational spin, accosting her as one pilot to another "On this wondrous sea / sailing silently" and exhorting Susan to "Write! Comrade, write!" toward a mutual Eternity "In the peaceful west." When, around summer 1858, she bound another copy of "On this wondrous sea" into Fascicle 1, Dickinson deepened the poem's vocational resonance by associating it with a more complex rendering of the same metaphor:

> Adrift! A little boat adrift!
> And night is coming down!
> Will *no* one guide a little boat
> Unto the nearest town?
> So sailors say – on yesterday –
> Just as the dusk was brown
> One little boat gave up it's strife
> And gurgled down and down.
> So angels say – on yesterday –
> Just as the dawn was red
> One little boat – o'erspent with gales
> Retrimmed it's masts – redecked it's sails –
> And shot – exultant on! (Fr 6A)

Unlike "On this wondrous sea," this poem explicitly presents struggle, loss, and distance from origins as the necessary preconditions for resurrection into a new condition. This boat's resurrection is invisible to the watching sailors, just as Dickinson's self-dedication to her poetic vocation may have been invisible to her social world (and so far as we know, she did not send this poem to Susan Dickinson or any other correspondent). Where the boats of "On this wondrous sea" sail toward their common destiny in a harbor where they will be eternally "at rest – / the anchors fast," this boat ends neither resting in port nor anchored, but rather running "exultant" with the wind. Perfunctory angels notwithstanding, the end of this journey is less an orthodox religious eternity than an aesthetic re-emergence of the little boat into a more colorful and active world, its final destination unknown.

Formally, the final stanza strikes off from its opening refrain into an emphatic rhymed couplet, adding an extra line to the quatrain, before ending with the off-rhyme of "on" with "down" and "down" and "brown"; at the same time, the literally repetitive and onomatopoetic, down-gurgling vocabulary of the first two stanzas opens into alliteration (a more generative form of repetition) and rises to the Latinate "exultant" (etymologically, "leaping up") in the poem's final three lines. It seems right to think of this poem as Dickinson's reflection on the launch of her fascicles: a literary event invisible to or wrongly understood by bystanders, perhaps one inaugurated with an act of selective destruction – killing off the fearful, self-diminishing diction of the poem's opening stanza so that another kind of poetry can begin to take its place.

Taken together, "On this wondrous sea" and "Adrift! A little boat adrift" are almost certainly among the earliest of Dickinson's surviving variant poems, to borrow Sharon Cameron's influential formulation: "Such poems do not exactly develop from each other so much as they repeat and modify aspects of each other."[22] The poems of loss, recompense, and exchange included in Fascicle 1 experiment with similar kinds of variation. "I had a guinea golden – / I lost it in the sand –" (Fr 12) begins one poem that goes on to itemize the further losses of "a crimson Robin" and a "Pleiad" in heaven. Another poem copied on the same sheet replies by pairing two similes in which a lack is met by with recompense out of all proportion to the original demand:

> As if I asked a common alms –
> And in my wondering hand,
> A stranger pressed a kingdom –
> And I – bewildered stand –
> As if I asked the Orient
> Had it for me a morn?
> And it sh'd lift it's purple dikes
> And flood me with the Dawn!   (Fr 14A)

Mabel Loomis Todd speculates in her 1896 edition of Dickinson's poems that "I had a guinea golden" "may have had, like many others, a personal origin," perhaps as a rebuke to a friend tardy in his correspondence.[23] The poem's archness and mock-poetic diction echo the style of Dickinson's earliest surviving poems, her album and newspaper verse plucked from her familiar letters. Its inclusion in Fascicle 1, however, edges "I had a guinea golden" away from its social origins and toward the condition of ballad or fable, reminiscent of Henry David Thoreau's famous claim to have "long ago lost a hound, a bay horse, and a turtle dove," and to be seeking them still, in the opening chapter of *Walden*. In both "I had a guinea golden" and "As if I asked a common alms" the speaker remains outwardly still while others move about the world – but she is moving in the relationship *between* these two poems: out of an outworn style, and toward the "Orient."

Implicit in both these poems of exchange is the question of being recognized by others, a question that Dickinson made explicit some four years after the copying of Fascicle 1 when she included "As if I asked a common Alms" in her second letter to Higginson, which replied to his interest in her work with the declaration that "I have had few pleasures so deep as your opinion" and closed by asking him, famously, "will you be my Preceptor, Mr Higginson"? (*Letters* 256, June 7, 1862). Dickinson's artful self-presentation in her correspondence with Higginson has been the subject of much critical commentary, and I will not pause on it here except to observe that the problem of recognition – of whether a poetic vocation entails readers – was not first raised for Dickinson by the appearance of Higginson's "Letter to a Young Contributor" in the April 1862 *Atlantic Monthly*: it was a central problem for the beginning of the fascicles.

Concern for vocational (and social and erotic) recognition is very much alive in the organizing floral metaphor that dominates Fascicle 1, from its opening poem, "The Gentian weaves her fringes" (Fr 21) through "When Roses cease to bloom, Sir" and ending with "Nobody knows this little Rose" (Fr 11). Let me give any reader trying to suppress her impatience with this fascicle's apparent surfeit of conventional blossoms permission to abandon the effort: in Fascicle 1, the rose is Dickinson's figure for a vocation legible to all. *Everybody* knows this little rose –

> Nobody knows this little rose;
> It might a pilgrim be,
> Did I not take it from the ways,
> And lift it up to thee!   (*Fr 11A, 11. 1–4*)

– and the poem's printing in the August 2, 1858 *Springfield Daily Republican* under the title "To Mrs. –, with a Rose," with the further advice that it was "Surreptitiously communicated to The Republican," underscores the point that the little rose's supposed invisibility, its nominally private gift circulation, is produced with half an eye toward public "ways."

Although bound in the final position in Fascicle 1, "Nobody knows this little Rose" may, Franklin suggests, have been among the earliest of the fascicle's poems in date of composition and copying; its style and mode of address as well as its route to publication connect it to the few poems surviving from Dickinson's album and newspaper verse of the early 1850s. The floral poems in Fascicle 1 become more interesting as Dickinson begins to detach them from the Rose's conventional legibility. Copied on the same sheet as "Nobody knows this little Rose," the following poem places the rose in competition with other vocational possibilities:

> Garlands for Queens, may be –
> Laurels – for rare degree
> Of soul or sword –
> Ah – but remembering me –
> Ah – but remembering thee –
> Nature in chivalry –
> Nature in charity –
> Nature in equity –
> The Rose ordained!   (*Fr 10A*)

Thematically, this poem's preference for the rose over laurels and garlands sets mutual romantic passion over and against more public and collective forms of recognition. The triad of chivalry–charity–equity invokes the familiar Christian trinity of faith, hope, and charity

(I Corinthians 13) and echoes similar triads throughout Fascicle 1 and elsewhere in Dickinson's writing:

Blooming – tripping – flowing	(*Fr 19, Fascicle 1*)
Summer – Sister – Seraph!	(*Fr 22, Fascicle 1*)
A sepal – petal –and a thorn	(*Fr 25, Fascicle 1*)
Burglar! Banker – Father!	(*Fr 39, Fascicle 2*)

In the name of the Bee –
And of the Butterfly –
And of the Breeze – Amen!   (*Fr 23, Fascicle 1*)

In any of these triads, blasphemy is not far out of earshot. As Helen Vendler observes, "It is Dickinson's conviction of her intellectual and aesthetic authority that enables her to stand, however whimsically, against the church, and offer Nature as a better object of worship than the Trinity."[24] More generous than orthodox religious authority, Nature in "Garlands for Queens" licenses Dickinson's erotic and vocational emergence for an audience of at least one – a "thee" adequate to her own aesthetic authority.

In other floral poems of Fascicle 1, the implied audience for Dickinson's emerging blooms becomes narrower, or more indefinitely deferred, even as the poems' aesthetic vocabulary becomes wider. The lines she selected to copy and bind at the very beginning of Fascicle 1 frame this shift away from publicity:

The Gentian weaves her fringes –
The Maple's loom is red –
My departing blossoms
Obviate parade.   (*Fr 21A*)

Like "Adrift! A little boat adrift!" (Fr 6), this poem becomes flashier in diction (notably in its Latinate final line) as its subject vanishes from the public eye. Here and elsewhere in Fascicle 1 the showy rose gives way to more recessive, less predictable flowers – the gentian as well as the crocus, the columbine, the tulip, the anemone: flowers perhaps more likely to blossom in place than be presented as bouquets or dedicated in albums, flowers less overdetermined by received forms of social or romantic address.

> To lose – if One can find again –
> To miss – if One shall meet –
> The Burglar cannot rob – then –
> The Broker cannot cheat.
> So build the hillocks gaily –
> Thou little spade of mine
> Leaving nooks for Daisy
> And for Columbine –
> You and I the secret
> Of the Crocus know –
> Let us chant it softly –
> "*There* is no more snow"!　　　　　　　　　　(*Fr 30A*)

Unlike Dickinson's lost "guinea golden," these flowers return to her seasonally, with their loss and return to some degree under the poet's control. The gardener setting out more bulbs and perennials than she can keep track of hopes to be pleasantly surprised come the spring. Along with the tulip sleeping "beneath a tree – / Remembered but by me" in another poem of this fascicle (Fr 15), the flowers of this poem share the capacity to delight the gardener with the delayed revelation of her own craft.

　　Dickinson's "little spade" arraying her garden is also, of course, her pen. For all their other differences, the same metaphor a century later organizes Seamus Heaney's famous poem of twentieth-century vocational emergence, "Digging." Published in Heaney's first book of poems, *Death of a Naturalist* (1966), "Digging" shows the poet surveying the distance between his work and that of his father, as seen both in the present, in which Heaney overlooks his father's "straining rump among the flowerbeds," and in memory, as Heaney recalls him planting potatoes. Acknowledging that "I've no spade to follow men" like his father and grandfather before him, Heaney takes up his own vocation in terms that claim both separation from and connection with his origins: "Between my finger and my thumb / The squat pen rests. / I'll dig with it."[25] Dickinson's poem by contrast represents the work of genteel ornamental gardening as continuous with her poetic vocation – as aesthetic craft rather than subsistence labor; her poem's distance from the physical necessity and other historical burdens patent in Heaney's "Digging" makes it in every sense a lighter work. Nevertheless, the world of her poem, like Heaney's, is divided between inside and outside, the father's realm and the poet's, although with the assignments reversed: where Heaney watches his father's labor in the garden from indoors, Dickinson has left her father's house for the work of her garden. Unlike Heaney's solid, straining working-class father, both house and father in Dickinson's poem are materially absent but defined by negation, in terms of the bourgeois patriarch's fears for his home: the burglars who steal, the brokers who undermine its financial foundation. For both Dickinson and Heaney, taking up the spade/pen distances them from the authority of their fathers, but only so far. Acknowledging that authority, and its continuing claims on them, will remain a burden for both poets.

Burglar, broker; "Burglar! Banker – Father!" (Fr 39): the associational trail leads back not only to Dickinson's human father but also to the other absent patriarch of the Dickinson Homestead, the Father of orthodox Christianity. *Where*, exactly, is there "no more snow"? Dickinson's poem admits of an orthodox religious reading, in which the seasonal resurrection of the crocus typifies the Christian afterlife, or a heterodox reading, in which Dickinson's art conspires with nature to compete with heaven. Looking ahead to other Dickinson poems may bias my reading of "To lose – if One can find again –"; still, I think the heterodox reading of this early poem is more compelling. Dickinson's "little spade" cultivates not the lily, the traditional floral symbol of resurrection, but rather the common crocus. Setting out plants where she can lose them in order to find them again, Dickinson makes light of the fears of loss and damnation that drive the religion of the burglar and the broker. As a reflection on vocational beginnings, this poem – like

"Adrift! A little boat adrift!" – embraces loss in order to realize a heterodox resurrection. It sets aside fear for the sake of *work*.

Of all Dickinson's manuscript books, Fascicle 1 is the most tightly bound to its dominant cluster of metaphors and the least distant from its social origin and formal model in the young lady's album-"garland" of poems. The extent to which later fascicles are organized around dominant metaphors and themes, or even entire narrative sequences, remains a matter of critical debate. Some scholars now believe – plausibly, in my view – that poems copied onto a single stationery sheet are more likely to cluster in a meaningful way than are all the poems on the several sheets that Dickinson typically bound into any one fascicle.[26] It seems to me that as Dickinson continued to assemble the fascicles, her model for their internal structure became looser, less tied to overt continuity of metaphor, and more invested in subtler kinds of variation and connection, even as she continued to elaborate on techniques explored from the very earliest of the fascicles. Sharon Cameron observes, for example, that "In several of the fascicles the first and last poem are either complementary or antithetical,"[27] a pattern that begins in Fascicle 1 with the organizing metaphor contrasting the gentian with the rose. Dickinson's practice of transcribing variant readings for individual words in poems copied into the fascicles seems to begin around 1861, especially in Fascicles 12–14. Variant poems, on the other hand – like the variant roses and boats of Fascicle 1 – characterize the fascicles from their inception, both within individual fascicles and across their boundaries, as when the "Burglar" and "Broker" of Fascicle 1 (Fr 30) return as "Burglar! Banker – Father!" in Fascicle 2 (Fr 39), or when "Wild nights – Wild Nights!" (Fr 269, Fascicle 11) finds an erotic solution, "Rowing in Eden," to the dichotomy between safe harbor and exploration posed by the boat poems of Fascicle 1. When Dickinson unlooses her earliest floral garlands, the principle of variation is what remains.

Nor did variation and conversation among poems end in Dickinson's work when she left behind the vocational project signaled by the fascicles. That long arc extends from the beginning of her career until its end, across the many various kinds of manuscript embodiments in which Dickinson's work descends to us. What matters about her poems is not just that they are copied in different manuscript formats at different times in her life and for different readers; what matters is that the poems themselves formally articulate Dickinson's changing conception of her poetic project over time. Witness the return of Fascicle 1's gentian in a poem transcribed and bound into Fascicle 24, around spring 1863:

> God made a little Gentian –
> It tried – to be a Rose –
> And failed – and all the Summer laughed –
> But just before the Snows
>
> There rose a Purple Creature
> That ravished all the Hill –
> And Summer hid her Forehead –
> And Mockery – was still –
>
> The Frosts were her condition –
> The Tyrian would not come
> Until the North – invoke it –
> Creator – Shall I – bloom?   (Fr 520A)

This poem condenses the dialogue among the various flower poems of Fascicle 1 into a single Cinderella story of poetic vocation: the late-blooming gentian aims and fails at conventional forms of social, romantic, and poetic legibility, only to see her "Tyrian" regal status revealed with the advent of winter (the Mediterranean city of Tyre was the ancient world's major source for a scarce and expensive purple dye associated with royalty). Wind and breath are traditional figures for poetic inspiration; Dickinson personifies them in this poem as a chilly, powerful, polar lover-muse of New England winter, bringing the gentian to life while shriveling the frailer blooms around her. "God made a little Gentian" offers a more powerful and contrarian figure of nature as the poet's ally than do the floral poems of Fascicle 1. As in so many of her poems of vocational emergence, the diction of this poem enacts the poem's theme, rising in sophistication from the first stanza's "little" vocabulary to the Latinate, allusive, intellectually evocative verbal resources of the final stanza. Frost is the gentian's "condition," as in the Kantian philosophical sense of autumn's providing the necessary conditions of possibility for the gentian's emergence into bloom; and perhaps also in a legalistic sense, as in a contractual condition that must be satisfied before the gentian will perform her part of a bargain with the North.

When she copied out "God made a little Gentian" in 1863, Dickinson may have believed that the vocational emergence it envisions for the late-blooming gentian was within her reach. She had made her outreach to Higginson the year before and had engaged his interest in her poems enough to sustain the correspondence, if not to make him her advocate for their publication. The *Springfield Republican* had printed "Safe in their alabaster chambers" (Fr 124A) in March 1862, perhaps with Susan Dickinson's aid and encouragement, and the spring of 1864 would mark the high point of publication during her lifetime, with five poems appearing in the *Republican* and elsewhere, several of them in multiple periodical venues. "Shall I – Bloom?": there is little reason to think that the question of an appropriate audience was sheerly rhetorical for Dickinson at this time, and equally little reason, I believe, for readers today to think of print publication as antithetical to the literary value of Dickinson's poems of these years.

At some point in Dickinson's life, this openness to publication seems to have shut down – the exact moment and motivation for the change being as hard to locate as her decision, at some point in the late 1850s, to inaugurate the fascicles. The gentian of Dickinson's late style is beautifully indifferent to questions of audience, status, and permanence:

> The Gentian has a parched Corolla –
> Like Azure dried
> 'Tis Nature's buoyant juices
> Beatified –
> Without a vaunt or sheen

As casual* as Rain   *odorless – *innocent
And as benign –
When most is past – it comes –
Nor isolate it seems –
It's Bond it's Friend –
To fill it's Fringed career
And aid an aged year
Abundant end –

It's lot – were it forgot –
This truth endear* –   * declare
Fidelity is gain
Creation o'er –   (*Fr 1458A, circa 1877*)

Like "The Mushroom is the Elf of Plants," this poem is a self-con-sciously late *ars poetica*, a poem that twines a meditation on human bodily aging and Dickinson's evolving, ever-revised aesthetic com-mitments around a deeply familiar organizing botanical metaphor. Rejecting "vaunt or sheen," this late flower is long past the earlier gentian's Cinderella fantasy of emerging to "ravish" a waiting audi-ence. It inhabits the world casually, indifferent to claiming space or to the prospect of being forgotten, as indifferent and benign as the rain that falls on the just and the unjust alike. Where Dickinson once boasted of poetry's ability to crush an enduring attar out of the ephem-eral rose ("Essential Oils are wrung –" [Fr 772, circa 1863]), this poem celebrates a poetry that is less invasive, to the point of being "odor-less" (in the variant Dickinson tried for "casual") – but only as odor-less as rain, releasing earthy scents without bearing any marked essence of its own.

Both the poem's form and its manuscript embodiment, in this instance, underline its thematic import. Dickinson's verse here is unusually varied, almost odic in its freedom, alternating lines of three stresses with two-stressed lines that bear understated emphasis and grouping them in stanzas that do not settle clearly into quatrains until the poem's end. Her rhyming is also unusually free, with three off-rhymes in sheen/rain/benign binding together lines 5–7, followed by a conspicuously tight *abba* grouping of perfect rhymes (ll. 10–13), then loosening again for the off-rhymes of the final quatrain. The poem's form seems unafraid of making overt thematic statements and equally unafraid of formal exploration. Its verse form develops as if faithful to itself, faithful to the "Bond" generated by its own writing.

By 1877, Dickinson had authored a "bond" of thousands of poems archived in her own keeping "Like Azure dried," in addition to the hundreds, at least, she sent to her correspondents. That archive may have been on her mind when, in this poem, she seems to affirm that keeping faith with one's past writing is as important or gainful as new creation. Although free and exploratory in its poetic form, this late work does not celebrate the unconditioned freedom of the blank page or the solitary flower. Written on the back of a note from her brother Austin addressed to "the old folks at home" – Dickinson and her sister Vinnie – this poem exemplifies Holland Cotter's verdict that Dickinson chose to be inspired by, and to bring her late works into being on, "paper that already carried words, familiar names and addresses. It was stained with life." Perhaps Austin's valetudinarian note, making various requests of his sisters for a "nice" dinner menu, prompted Dickinson to write a poem reaffirming where her life's real work lay. Her poem's value to us lies in its aesthetic realization of a human life lived in time and a poetic vocation in tune with the aging body, one that asserts its earned autonomy without pomposity, vaunt, or sheen, or need of "isolate" detachment from other human frailties and fidelities.

2   Some striding – Giant – Love –

In Todd and Higginson's 1890 volume of Dickinson's poems, Book II, "Love," comprising eighteen poems, follows directly upon "Life." Aside from a couple of pieces in Dickinson's early floral gift-idiom and one late poem probably sent to Mabel Loomis Todd, almost all of these poems were transcribed into Dickinson's manuscript books, her present-day editors believe, between 1861 and 1865, her most concentrated period of poetic production. A few were also shared in her letters, but for many of them the fascicle copy is unique; so far as the surviving record can tell us, Dickinson did not share many of these poems with other readers during her lifetime, and no one correspondent seems to have been singled out consistently to receive those she did share. For readers who believe that something uniquely valuable about Dickinson's writings inheres in their direct, concrete address to familiar individual correspondents, these poems considered as a group provide no such hook on which to hang an account of why they matter. Yet I would wager that these poems – among them "Mine by the Right of the White Election" (Fr 411), "I cannot live with you" (Fr 706), "There came a day at summer's full (Fr 325), "I'm ceded – I've stopped being theirs" (Fr 353), "T'was a long parting, but the time / for Interview had come" (Fr 691) and "I'm Wife – I've finished that –" (Fr 225) – remain some of Dickinson's most important, across many communities of readers. And for every poem Todd and Higginson included in "Love," readers could supply examples of many more inhabiting the same structure of feeling.

It is hard to settle for calling this generative structure, which looms so large in Dickinson's oeuvre, simply "love." Not that Dickinson herself didn't use the word, and frequently; but to compare one of her definitional or riddling poems about love, such as "While it is alive" (Fr 287) or "Struck was I nor yet by lightning" (Fr 841), with her contemporary Elizabeth Barrett Browning's celebration of "love, mere love" in *Sonnets from the Portuguese* is to see how far Dickinson will go not to wallow in tautology.[1] Dickinson's love poems are inextricably entangled with poems of vocational self-formation and of longing for recognition writ more broadly, as well as with poems skeptical about the received social forms of committed love, especially for women. She writes of ecstasy and fidelity, but also of deeply painful experiences and affects attached to thwarted desire: not just renunciation, which may offer some compensation in acknowledged mutual feeling and ethical agency, but also humiliation and social invisibility. Whatever the predominant gender, if there was one, of Dickinson's biographical object choices, it is Dickinson's writing of thwarted and invisible desire that makes her poetry – in the useful shorthand of our own day – queer.

Barrett Browning's sonnets form a coherent narrative sequence, and, moreover, one addressed to a beloved whose identity was transparent to her readership. Dickinson's love poems, however persistent their return to certain situations and problems, do not. Efforts to extract a singular, literal autobiographical narrative from the love poems of Dickinson's fascicles, such as William Shurr's in *The Marriage of Emily Dickinson*, come to grief on their determination to read Dickinson's metaphors literally and her speakers as reliably identical with Dickinson herself: thus, Shurr's Dickinson has a love child somehow both born and aborted, a marriage both renounced and consummated.[2] Although extreme in its urgency and literalism, Shurr's need to attach the felt intensity of Dickinson's love poems to biographical experience of one kind or another is shared by many readers, myself included, and not easily dismissed. I don't think we can fully appreciate the value of Dickinson's central writings on love from this part of her career – her poems as well as the famous, shattering three "Master" letters of the fascicle years (*Letters* 187, 233, 248) – without acknowledging how difficult it is to tolerate the uncertainty in which they leave us about their biographical referents.

Absent biographical grounding, these poems open a potentially boundless space for fantasy in erotic life. Just how autonomous can desire be? What, if anything, does it require of a concrete other and of a social surround? Dickinson's writings on love pose just these questions, often in powerfully abstracted, almost algebraic forms. "Of all the Souls that stand create – / I have Elected – One," begins one poem that ends with the imperative, "Behold the Atom – I preferred – / To all the lists of Clay!" (Fr 279A, circa 1862). The "Atom" of this strange love poem lacks every possible identifying attribute, including gender; it is a bare mathematical unit, "One" against many. Some of her readers, Paula Bennett most notably,[3] have looked to give this featureless, indivisible "Atom" a local habitation and a name by calling Dickinson's aesthetic autoerotic or masturbatory; but this seems only a different way of trying to pin down the referents that the poems themselves deny their present-day readers, rather than valuing their power on their own terms.

If Dickinson's poems of love, passion, and yearning do not tender readers a coherent autobiographical narrative, the surviving manuscript record nevertheless allows at least the bare outlines of a story to be told about their writing. Certain ways of writing poetry about love and desire seem to have had a beginning for Dickinson around 1860, an ebbing after the mid-1860s, and a self-conscious ending in the early 1870s. When Dickinson writes of love in her poetry after the early 1870s – and, of course, she does – she often seems to be musing about what it means to write in the afterlife of this great period of romantic and professional possession. The questions posed in many of the earlier love poems – Must desire be addressed to a concrete other? What does it require by way of response from the other and of the surrounding social world? – resonate and overlap with the more clearly vocational questions of Dickinson's early work: How autonomous can my poetry be? Does it require a concrete addressee, or a yet broader audience? Dickinson's love poems, then, are central to the kind of literary value I have identified with the life of Dickinson's writing and the development of her style and themes, early and late.

Borrowing the poet James Merrill's words (which he borrowed in turn from Northrop Frye), this chapter explores this long arc in Dickinson's poetry as a mythic plot, "an old, exalted one: / the incarnation and withdrawal of / A god" more than as provocation to literal biographical speculation.[4] Although Dickinson eschews Merrill's or Frye's syncretic range of reference, the proximity of their old, exalted plots to Christianity's sacred narrative of incarnation, passion, and redemption is very near to Dickinson's purposes in many of these famous poems, in which human love models itself on this sacred plot; is taken up into it; competes with it; is forbidden by it. In all her variations on this narrative, human passion yields Dickinson nothing by way of visible earthly recognition. Her love has no determinate addressee and no social audience; its recognition is deferred, if it comes at all, to the afterlife in which she steals Pontius Pilate's famous words in the New Testament, *ecce homo* – "Behold the man," Jesus Christ (John 19.5, KVJ) – to celebrate, before the assembled heavenly hosts of the Resurrection, her irrevocable election of her irreducibly mysterious "Atom."

However this exalted narrative of passion ended for Dickinson in biographical terms, its withdrawal from the life of her writing left room for other developments. From the late 1870s until her death, the afterlife of this grand story encompassed the one overwhelming erotic interest of Dickinson's life whose identity is well attested in her surviving writings: Judge Otis Lord, a family friend of her father's age living in Salem, Massachusetts, to whom she addressed a number of surviving letters and impassioned drafts of letters that may or may not have been sent in another form. Some of these manuscripts were scissored and censored by hands unknown before they were eventually published as a group by Millicent Todd Bingham, Mabel Loomis Todd's niece, as *Emily Dickinson: A Revelation* (1954). Some are astonishing in their physical candor and verbal invention. "My lovely Salem smiles at me," begins one:

> I confess that I love him – I rejoice that I love him – I thank the maker of Heaven and Earth – that gave him me to love – the exultation floods me – I cannot find my channel – The Creek turns Sea – at thought of thee –. . . .
>   Incarcerate me in yourself – rosy penalty – threading with you this lovely maze, which is not Life or Death – though it has the intangibleness of one, and the flush of the other – waking for your sake on Day made magical with you before I went (*Letters* 559, circa 1878)

Strikingly, however, almost no formally realized poems are known to have emerged out of this flood of feeling and writing. Franklin's edition of Dickinson's poetry distills just three short poems out of draft manuscripts thought to be intended for Lord (Fr 1477, 1557, 1622, transcribed from about 1878 to 1882), none of great power. "I cannot find my channel" indeed: in the writings connected to Lord, Dickinson's rhythm and rhyme abort, the formal structures of poetry dissolve, and the willful self celebrated in many of the earlier love poems recedes.

Interest in Dickinson's vivid, fragmentary late writings associated with Otis Lord has increased over the years, driven on the one hand by a string of high-profile biographies, most recently Lyndall Gordon's *Lives Like Loaded Guns* (2010), that rate Lord's importance in Dickinson's emotional life highly, and on the other hand by manuscript scholars such as Marta Werner who attach high aesthetic value to these formally open, visually arresting scraps and mutilated pages. Here Werner's online edition of and commentary on these manuscripts – *Ravished Slates: Revisioning the "Lord" Letters* – is well worth exploring. As the scare quotes of Werner's title intimate, she and other critics who treasure these manuscripts as "witnesses of Dickinson's late experimental writing"[5] often discount their biographical association with Lord, for reasons as much concerned with theories of aesthetic value as with proper editorial caution about assuming that these diverse manuscripts stem from a single biographical inspiration or occasion. The highly experimental, visually oriented, and strenuously autonomous aesthetic value Werner locates in these late writings leads her to read them as "outside all forms of address and signature"[6] rather than as writings inspired by and addressed (even in imagination) to the jowly, aging man of Lord's surviving photographs who, like Dickinson's father, dedicated his life to service of the law.

To my mind, though, it makes almost as little sense, biographically or aesthetically, to obfuscate the address to Lord in the most arresting of these writings as it does to try to supply a proper name for Dickinson's "Atom" in her poems of the 1860s. Dickinson's wordplay on Lord's name and his legal vocation in these writings, her luxuriant

exploration of unfamiliar rhetorical positions (writing as the acknowledged beloved, the pursued as much as the pursuer) – all these aesthetic
moves exploit the writings' biographical address to Lord. Still, the lesson
of Dickinson's "Atom" remains active in the manuscripts associated
with Lord: desire, even reciprocated desire, is never fully determined or
exhausted by its object. As Werner rightly stresses, "Addressed to an
absent other, lost the moment it is sent, the love letter is a figure of the
wanderer or the deviant."[7] In the gesture of inviting Judge Lord to
"incarcerate" her deviance, Dickinson transforms the proper name
"Lord" into an evocative word, a liberating figure of possibility (a jail
to break open), and a muse of her late writing – not just the stolid pillar of
the community living in Salem, Massachusetts.

As I observed earlier, very little formally ordered poetry seems to
have come from the exploratory writings that Dickinson addressed to
Lord, or to "Lord." Apart from these writings, however, Dickinson did
produce a valuable body of late poems – some shared with Susan
Dickinson, some with other correspondents, some kept in her own
papers – that lay claim to her authority to write of love to particular
correspondents as well as in general, even impersonal terms. "Till it
has loved, no man or woman can become itself," she wrote to Thomas
Wentworth Higginson in late 1878, congratulating him after reading a
newspaper report of his second marriage (*Letters* 575). Without volun-
teering to him any direct revelation of her personal experience, her
letter demands that Higginson acknowledge the authority of her language; accept her oblique, unconventional blessing on his conventionally public union; and respect in turn her implicit claim to have
undergone love's rigorous trial of self-fashioning outside of any such
singular, socially legible relationship. Early and late, Dickinson's
writings of love continue to make the same demands of her readers
in the present day.

One of Dickinson's most famous and fully elaborated early love
poems encapsulates the incarnation and withdrawal of a god – love,
Eros – within the space of a single summer day:

> There came a Day at Summer's full,
> Entirely for me –

I thought that such were for the Saints,
Where Resurrections – be –

The Sun, as common, went abroad,
The flowers, accustomed, blew,
As if no soul the solstice passed
That maketh all things new –

The time was scarce profaned, by speech –
The symbol of a word
Was needless, as at Sacrament,
The Wardrobe, of our Lord –

Each was to each The Sealed Church,
Permitted to commune, this – time –
Lest we too awkward show
At supper of the Lamb.

The Hours slide fast – as Hours will,
Clutched tight, by greedy hands –
So faces on two Decks, look back,
Bound to opposing lands –

And so when all the time had leaked,
Without external sound
Each bound the Other's Crucifix –
We gave no other Bond –

Sufficient Troth, that we shall rise –
Deposed – at length, the Grave –
To that new Marriage,
Justified – through Calvaries – of Love –   (*Fr 325D, circa 1862*)

This great poem is so well known that it may be difficult to focus on
how eccentric and original it is considered as a love poem. Until the
fourth stanza, there is no "we" in the poem, and not until the fifth

stanza does that "we" explicitly become a "we" of two, a romantic couple. The same simile that finally reveals them as a couple also announces their separation, as the lovers on this summer's day confront one another like "faces on two Decks... / Bound to opposing lands." The poem's confident opening assertion of a momentous arrival, struck home by the first stanza's emphatically regular iambic meter and perfect rhyme, contrasts with the poem's artful lack of definition as to *who* arrived, and how and at what moment. Like the "Atom" in "Of all the Souls that stand create," the romantic other of this poem lacks every kind of social specification, even down to gender – not an easy matter to hold in abeyance in a poem structured as a first-person narrative of an event, where gendered pronouns would be conventional and expected as they are not in a second-person address (*he came* or *she came* versus *you came*). Dickinson modulates the poem's initial first-person singular pronouns – I/me – into the first-person plural *we* without any intervening notation of the romantic partner as a separate human person. Literally speaking, the only thing that comes with certainty to the speaker in this poem is the day of the summer solstice, arriving "entirely for *me*" rather than as something granted to an expectant human couple. Taking the poem at its own word, then, and following Northrup Frye and James Merrill into the register of myth, we might simply call Dickinson's beloved of this poem a solar god: the incarnation of the solstice sun, the "man of noon" (as she named him in a famous letter of 1852 to Susan Gilbert, *Letters* 93).

Nature generously grants Dickinson this visitation on the longest day of the year even while the poem's orthodox Christian God insists that it is only a practice session, one day's bliss conceded as rehearsal for the delayed gratification deferred to heaven. The lovers nominally accede to their separation, exchanging crucifixes as their only witness to the day and their only sign of their faith in one another. As Helen Vendler points out, however, Dickinson turns their notional obedience toward blasphemy. The poem's conclusion, in which "the lovers' crucifixions replicate in identical detail that of Jesus," his Calvary becoming their calvaries, "confirms her defiance of the conventional God."[8] Long by Dickinson's standards, "There came a Day at Summer's full" like a magnificent overture adumbrates situations and figures that Dickinson wrote variations on throughout the early 1860s: proclaiming herself "Wife – without the Sign! / Empress of Calvary" (Fr 194, circa 1861); reciting Christ's and her own "scalding" prayer, "Sabacthani," at her private Gesthemane of renunciation (Fr283C, circa 1863); imagining a reunion with her beloved's dead body, when at last "I and Thee / Permitted – face to face to be – " can look back "At those Old Times – in Calvary" (Fr 431, circa 1862); imagining a reunion with the resurrected lover, claimed as her own before the entire assembled host of the Resurrection (Fr 279); or concluding bleakly that neither life nor death nor even resurrection can unite her with the beloved,

> Because You saturated sight –
> And I had no more eyes
> For sordid excellence
> As Paradise   (*Fr 706A, circa 1863*)

Individually and as a group, these poems constitute not just a record of private lament, but rather an extended project of personal myth-making within the grandest narratives of Dickinson's culture.

The British second-generation Romantic and Victorian poets who were Dickinson's precursors and near-contemporaries had recourse to fully elaborated classical worlds when they set about writing some of their most ambitious poetry – Keats's *Hyperion* and *Fall of Hyperion*, Shelley's *Prometheus Unbound*. In Dickinson's ambitious love poems of the 1860s, Prometheus is a woman, issuing her defiance from the summer garden or the domestic parlor rather than the desolate crag where Prometheus was chained. Without taking on the outward trappings of the classical tradition, Dickinson finds in the Christian narrative of Calvary, as Linda Freedman observes, a means of "forg[ing] the connection between the Greek demi-god [Prometheus] and the Christian God incarnate."[9] Dickinson claims godlike powers for human love and abides the torture that follows:

> I got so I could walk across
> That Angle in the floor,

> Where he turned so, and I turned – how –
> And all our Sinew tore -   (*Fr 292A, ll. 5–8, circa 1862*)

Marriage, according to the Bible, unites two persons as "one flesh" (Mark 10:8). Here Dickinson's unorthodox yoking of the singular noun *sinew* to the first-person plural *our* implies that the lovers separated in this poem were previously one flesh: once united in a marriage, however unorthodox, and now enduring the agony of one flesh becoming two. Experimenting with the opening line of this poem – set down first, in Fascicle 12, as "I got so I could hear his name" – Dickinson eventually underlined an alternative reading: "I got so I could take his name –":

> I got so I could hear˙ his name –   * think • take
> Without – Tremendous gain –
> That Stop-sensation – on my soul –
> And Thunder – in the Room –   (*Fr 292A, ll. 1–4*)

Behind this stanza, unvoiced but invoked in its rhyme, looms the commandment of the Decalogue against taking the name of God in vain (Exodus 20.7) as well as the social convention of the bride assuming her husband's name. The beloved whose name she never took in a recognized earthly marriage usurps the place of God in her cosmos, "stands for Deity" to her, as the following poem in the fascicle proclaims, and even in their separation remains to her the incarnation of a

> striding – Giant – Love –
>
> So greater than the Gods can show,
> They slink before the Clay,
> That not for all their Heaven can boast
> Will let it's Keepsake – go   (*Fr 293A, ll. 16–20, circa 1862*)

Her love itself (notably, this poem's pronoun for the beloved is "it") is the Promethean giant whose single-minded fidelity shames the Gods, the Olympians of classical mythology as well as the jealous God of Dickinson's Christian upbringing.

The giant ambitions of this poem and others like it are vocational as well as erotic. Dickinson signaled as much when she selected "There came a Day at Summer's full" as one of three poems she enclosed in her second letter to Thomas Wentworth Higginson, after her first approach elicited both his curiosity and, famously, what she called his "surgery"; presumably she thought this poem's mythography impersonal and elevated enough to stand alongside "Of all the Sounds despatched abroad" (Fr 334), also enclosed with this letter, another long poem by Dickinson's standards and one she may have hoped Higginson could recognize as an adaptation of high romantic nature odes (*Letters* 261). Perhaps Higginson grasped the vocational dimension of this and similar poems; certainly readers since Higginson have had little difficulty interpreting poems such as "I'm ceded—I've stopped being Their's" (Fr 353) and "Mine – by the Right of the White Election" (Fr 411), both included in the "Love" section of Higginson and Todd's 1890 *Poems*, as witnessing Dickinson's marriage to her art rather than to a literal human lover. "I'm ceded" deploys all the social and sacramental trappings of marriage to consecrate its speaker's change of state:

> I'm ceded – I've stopped being Their's –
> The name They dropped opon my face
> With water, in the country church
> Is finished using, now,
> And They can put it with my Dolls,
> My childhood, and the string of spools,
> I've finished threading – too –
>
> Baptized, before, without the choice,
> But this time, consciously, Of Grace –
> Unto supremest name –
> Called to my Full – The Crescent dropped –
> Existence's whole Arc, filled up,
> With one – small Diadem –
>
> My second Rank – too small the first –
> Crowned – Crowing – on my Father's breast –

> A half unconscious Queen –
> But this time – Adequate – Erect,
> With Will to choose,
> Or to reject,
> And I choose, just a Crown –   (*Fr 353A, circa 1862*)

The tiara, the father giving away the bride, the taking of a new name, the orthodox religious and social sequence of sacraments from baptism to matrimony, girlhood to womanhood: everything is here except, conspicuously, the bridegroom. Invited, as it seems, to witness one familiar rite, readers experience something else unfolding, as over the course of the poem's three stanzas the speaker moves from naming herself as the object of others' actions – being *ceded, baptized, called* – to claiming, "Erect" and "adequate" unto herself, a power of choice that may or may not require another human being as its object. The object of the speaker's imperative claim in "Mine – by the Right of the White Election!" is equally indeterminate:

> Mine – by the Right of the White Election!
> Mine – by the Royal Seal!
> Mine – by the Sign in the Scarlet prison –
> Bars – cannot conceal!
>
> Mine – here – in Vision – and in Veto!
> Mine – by the Grave's Repeal –
> Titled – Confirmed –
> Delirious Charter!
> Mine – long as Ages steal!   (*Fr 411A, circa 1862*)

Dickinson's range of metaphor in this short poem invokes the whiteness of the marriage veil, of virginity, of the blank page; the scarlet of a flush, of hymenal blood, and (as Elizabeth Phillips points out) of a famous letter in American fiction, sewn on the breast of a woman imprisoned for adultery.[10] In another, more strained and less accomplished, poem written around the same time, Dickinson hopes for possession of her beloved's dead body ("If I may have it, when it's dead," Fr 431). In this poem, by contrast, the body she claims is first and foremost her own. In pallor, in flush and in blood, hers is the power to write the desire written on and in her body.

The vocational claims made by Dickinson's poems of passion, possession, and recognition are extraordinarily powerful. At the same time, something vital is lost, I believe, in reading these poems *only* in vocational terms. Although such readings usefully deflect interpretive speculation about the biographical referents of the poems, they also leach away the identity of the writing body with the desiring body, the identity so absolutely affirmed in "Mine – by the Right of the White Election." They diminish the risks taken by a poem such as "I'm ceded – I've stopped being Their's," which dares its readers to imagine a woman standing at the altar, no husband in waiting, as a Queen. "Till it has loved, no man or woman can become itself": these great poems mine the seam where love and work merge in the human project of self-fashioning.

The risk entertained by these poems is that the vocational and erotic self fashioned with such labor will be received as either monstrous or invisible, or – in the worst instance – as both. The following astonishing poem, copied into Fascicle 11 around 1861,[11] takes that risk further than any other poem Dickinson wrote.

> Rearrange a "Wife's" Affection!
> When they dislocate my Brain!
> Amputate my freckled Bosom!
> Make me bearded like a man!
>
> Blush, my spirit, in thy Fastness –
> Blush, my unacknowledged clay –
> Seven years of troth have taught thee
> More than Wifehood ever may!
>
> Love that never leaped it's socket –
> Trust intrenched in narrow pain –

Constancy thro' fire – awarded –
Anguish – bare of anodyne!

Burden – borne so far triumphant –
None suspect me of the crown,
For I wear the "Thorns" till *Sunset* –
Then – my Diadem put on.

Big my Secret but it's *bandaged* –
It will never get away
Till the Day it's weary Keeper
Leads it through the Grave to thee.   (*Fr 267A, circa late 1861*)

This poem has been read as evidence of a secret marriage, a pregnancy, and perhaps an abortion; alternatively, as an exploration of a same-sex union between women "that is improper, unrecognized, yet more substantive than the conventional form of marriage."[12] As with so many of Dickinson's poems about desire and passion, however, "Rearrange a 'Wife's' Affection" offers readers nothing at all in the way of biographical information about the object of Dickinson's desire. The fundamental subject of this poem, I think – and the subject as well of the two urgent "Master" letters written by Dickinson around the same time (*Letters* 233, 248) – is shame. This poem's perversely "triumphant," self-wounding accomplishment lies in achieving social invisibility for its speaker's desiring body. Were her discipline ever to lapse, were her "unacknowledged clay" exposed to the gaze of the world, the speaker would stand revealed in a body grotesque, even freakish: a bandaged gravid woman, her bosom bared for radical surgery, her face flushed with desire and her desire perhaps inviting still more shaming interventions – "Make me bearded like a man!"

Whatever the biographical referents of Dickinson's poem, it seems inevitable and right that readers in our own day should value "Rearrange a 'Wife's' Affection" as a powerful entry in the canon of what David Halperin and Valerie Traub call "gay shame," or even, more recently, as a contribution to the literature of disability.[13] A love that dare not speak its name; a desire whose revelation would unsex its owner; an open secret, big but bandaged, whose management is the ceaseless burden of daily life and whose revelation feels both forbidden and compulsory – Dickinson's poem misses no element of what Eve Kosofsky Sedgwick so memorably christened the "epistemology of the closet."[14] It is also worth remembering, however, that in Dickinson's historical milieu a woman's desire did not have to be unorthodox in the gender of its object choices to be profoundly shaming. Dickinson would have had to look no further than one of her favorite authors, Charlotte Brontë, to find both a brilliant series of literary works and an ugly body of *ad feminam* biographical commentary testifying to what Laura Morgan Green calls a "particularly female form of humiliation" in mid-Victorian Anglo-American life and letters: the humiliation attending "the abject status of the single woman or the even more shameful status of an unrequitedly desirous one," and attached as well to the author who committed these humiliating affects to writing.[15] As the "Master" letters demonstrate, Dickinson could – and, at least on those occasions, did – explore the shaming epistemology of the closet in writing addressed to a man.[16]

Assuming Franklin's dating of "Rearrange a 'Wife's' Affection" to be accurate and the poem's internal timeline to bear some relation to biographical fact, the seven-year duration of Dickinson's "troth" – echoing Jacob's biblical seven years of service for Rachel (Genesis 29:20) – would locate the origin of Dickinson's "big" secret to about 1854. This year saw some of Dickinson's most intense and demanding correspondence with Susan Gilbert, probably including the famous undated letter in which Dickinson delivered Susan an emotional ultimatum – "you can go or stay" – along with her own avowal of their relationship's significance: "I have lived by this. It is the lingering emblem of the Heaven I once dreamed" (*Letters* 173). It was also in 1854 that Dickinson's early exchange of poems with Henry Emmons seems to have come to an end, as he was graduated from Amherst College and became engaged; and it was in 1854 that Dickinson wrote her last known letter to her childhood friend Abiah Root, also about to be married, in which she dwelt on having recently nursed Susan ("Susie, our dear friend") through a "Nervous Fever" and declined

Abiah's invitation to visit, telling her "I dont go from home, unless emergency leads me by the hand" (*Letters* 166). All told, Susan Dickinson seems a plausible candidate for the biographical object, if there was one unique object, of the heterodox "troth" that Dickinson plights in "Rearrange a 'Wife's' Affection"; yet the intensity of her relationship with Emmons also falls near in time to this poem's "Seven years of troth," and so too does Dickinson's presumed first encounter with the Reverend Charles Wadsworth during her visit to Philadelphia in the spring of 1855.[17] All that can be said with certainty is that the period of Dickinson's "troth" in this poem coincides with those obscure years in which she navigated the passage into her own poetic style and her adult style of life.

What can also be said with certainty is that someone was pregnant in 1861, but it was Susan Dickinson, not Emily, who was delivered of her first child, Edward (Ned) Dickinson, in June 1861. Whether or not Dickinson conceived of her "'Wife's' affection" as addressed specifically to Susan, the contrast between the social and sexual visibility of Susan's marriage to Austin and Dickinson's "unacknowledged clay" might never have been sharper for her than it was in the summer of 1861. That contrast alone may have more than sufficiently posed this poem's queer Hobson's choice between the only two possible outcomes for the speaker's desire: the condition of invisibility ("the abject status of the single woman," in Green's words) or that of a humiliating, unsexing exposure ("the even more shameful status of an unrequitedly desirous one"). Choosing where no socially legible choice is open to her, Dickinson recruits marriage and pregnancy as figures for this poem's aesthetic labor with erotic and vocational invisibility.

The hammering, imperative, and essentially unvaried trochaic meter (a trochee is a strong syllable followed by a weak syllable) of "Rearrange a 'Wife's' Affection," reinforced by the insistent alliteration chaining *brain* to *bosom* to *beard* to *body* to *burden*, underlines the poem's labored struggle to produce invisibility under conditions of choosing without choice. The speaker commands her body to bring forth her secret by doing what bodies do by themselves, involuntarily – blush, grow big with pregnancy – and at the same time requires this "big" body to keep her open secret "*bandaged*," giving a hostile or indifferent audience permission to ignore her burden without denying them the epistemological privilege (as Sedgwick would stress) of knowing it is there. Like "There came a Day at Summer's full," this poem is a compendium of Dickinson's repeated figures of passion – Calvary, marriage, crown – but one that obliquely acknowledges the social context and cost of embodying this personal myth, especially as a woman. If Prometheus were a woman, this poem implies, part of her daily agonies would include the concealment of them. "Rearrange a 'Wife's' affection" refuses to transubstantiate its "*bandaged*" condition into the "white sustenance" (in variant readings, "white exercise" or "white privilege") Dickinson derives from her pain at the end of "I cannot live with You –" (Fr 706). The speaker's nightly assumption of her "Diadem" does nothing here to sublimate the daily labor of her humiliating secret. The poem's conclusion imagines death and resurrection coming not as the triumphant revelation of Dickinson's most exalted versions of this story – *behold the atom I preferred!* – but rather as the "weary" transfer of a fractious burden (her heart "outgrew me – and like the little mother – with the big child – I got tired holding him," Dickinson writes in the second of the "Master" letters [*Letters* 233]) to an addressee who, like other fathers of bastard children in fact and fiction, may not take any great pleasure in its delivery. The desublimating impulse behind "Rearrange a 'Wife's' Affection" bares the shameful rag and bone shop from which Dickinson's most exalted personal myth of self-fashioning emerged.

Why Dickinson eventually wearied of this exalted myth is unknown and perhaps, at this distance, unknowable. What matters more are the beautiful traces of its withdrawal that she committed to writing. Linda Freedman points to the following short poem, the "one openly erotic poem," according to her biographer Habegger, that survives from Dickinson's lean years of 1866–1870, as "reflect[ing] her sense of the limitations of the Promethean urge:"[18]

The smouldering embers blush –
Oh Cheek within the Coal

Hast thou survived so many nights?
The smouldering embers smile –

Soft stirs the news of Light
The stolid Rafters glow
One requisite has Fire that Lasts
Prometheus never knew -   (Fr 1143A, circa 1868)

Like so many late Dickinson poems, this one returns to and revises elements of her earlier work. The blushing body of "Rearrange a 'Wife's affection," at once painfully exposed and "unacknowledged," returns here in a metaphor expressive of all the intimate warmth and reciprocity absent in the earlier poem. The poet blows on the coals of her banked fire, of a cold morning; returning to life, they return her smile. The daily return of fire in this poem signals domestic comfort rather than the annealing torment of "Constancy thro' fire – awarded –." In the poems of Dickinson's Promethean years, the unalterable sameness she asserts for her "striding – Giant – Love" is coupled with the unalterable sameness of its interdiction. What the poet here may know that Prometheus did not is that constancy itself, "Fire that lasts," can be variable; it sinks and returns. And in its nature, the "same" fire may not always be feeding on the same coal.

The later Dickinson attaches constant love to an aesthetic of renewal, revival, and accrual rather than a high heroic internal theater of fixed adversaries and irrevocable events. Where the characteristic plots of Dickinson's high theater of passion tend, as Helen Vendler observes, to compress "the multiple time-zones of 'normal' life into a crucial two: Before and After," what came before all the sinews tore and what came after, these later writings find "a stance that allows some form of continuing life"[19] – continuing life both for her love and for her writing. "The incidents of Love / Are more than it's Events," Dickinson wrote in a short quatrain that she both kept in a copy for herself and sent to Susan Gilbert Dickinson next door (Fr 1172, circa 1870). Some years later she returned once more to the question of what constitutes love's events, in another note sent to Susan Dickinson, probably in 1884, near the end of her life:

Morning might come by Accident – Sister –
Night comes by Event –
To believe the final line of the Card would foreclose Faith –
Faith is *Doubt*.

Sister –

Show me eternity, and I will show you Memory –
Both in one package lain
And lifted back again –
Be Sue – while I am Emily –
Be next – what you have ever been – Infinity –

(Letters 912, circa 1884; Fr 1658)

The theory of love embodied in this "letter-poem," as Ellen Louise
Hart and Martha Nell Smith aptly call it,[20] begins with the contrast
between the accidents of morning and the events of night.
Etymologically, accidents (from the Latin *ad*, "to," and *cadere*, "to
fall") are what befall us, whereas events (Latin *ex*, "out of" and *venire*,
"to come") emerge from what has come before. Love may begin as a
coup de foudre, an accident falling out of a clear blue sky; but love
becomes an event over time, which allows love's ongoing present to
emerge out of all that came before.

Another name for the temporal coherence of love's present with
its past, Dickinson offers, is "Faith." Love that begins as an unwilled
"Accident" may choose to become an event, may elect to keep faith
with its own past. Where Dickinson's earlier love poetry, however,
attaches fidelity to conditions of absolute, willed certainty – *Behold
the Atom I preferred!* – the late letter-poem identifies faith with
"*Doubt*." In the earlier poem, Dickinson's unchanging, featureless,
indivisible Atom gives up its identity in a singular moment of perfect
visual revelation; the difficult woman to whom Dickinson addressed
these late lines would never be so available to inspection. Given
Dickinson's history of eye troubles, perhaps she meant the "final
line of the Card" to invoke the Snellen vision chart, which came
into widespread use during her lifetime, or perhaps her reference is
to a closing line in some previous correspondence with Susan. In any
case, her metaphor concedes that the moment will never come when

the beloved other is revealed and known with finality. Love must put its faith where its doubt is, in lines that the eye cannot resolve.

When the lines of this letter-poem modulate into clearly rhymed verse, they assert that human "Memory" is equal, perhaps even superior, to orthodox religion's "eternity." Here Dickinson lays claim to the grand tradition of love poetry, invoking its vaunted power to immortalize the beloved, but very much on her own terms. As gracefully as they flatter Sue's own intrinsic "Infinity," hers without need of the poet's recognition, these lines also memorialize Dickinson's lifelong fidelity to her own writing – her lines laid away, lifted up, re-read and revised, commended to the scores of fascicle packets and hundreds of manuscript sheets that she preserved, in the faith and doubt that they would survive her.

3   Women, now, queens, now!

In his magisterial anthology *The Experience of Literature*, first issued in 1967 and intended for college-level literary courses, Columbia University's august literary critic Lionel Trilling included a poem by Emily Dickinson among the twenty-two works of poetry he selected for reprinting and explication. *The Experience of Literature* introduced Dickinson into very good company, alongside Milton's "Lycidas," Arnold's "Dover Beach," Keats's "Ode to a Nightingale," Marvell's "To His Coy Mistress," Shelley's "Ode to the West Wind," and Eliot's "The Waste Land," not to mention, elsewhere in the anthology, Sophocles's *Oedipus Rex* and Shakespeare's *King Lear* – a substantial vote of confidence in her value, especially for a poet whose works had only been available in something approaching a complete and reliable edition since 1955.

Trilling's principle of selection was anything but mysterious: allowing for the economies that dictated "Lycidas" over *Paradise Lost*, he represented major poets by one of their best-known works. Confronted with Dickinson's poetry, though, that principle appears to have broken down. Of the 1,775 poems before him in Thomas H. Johnson's 1955 variorum edition, Trilling lit upon an obscure short poem that had not drawn any previous editor's eye before *Bolts of Melody* (1945) gathered together the last bits of Dickinson's writing left unpublished in Mabel Loomis Todd's possession:

> "Go tell it"—What a Message—
> To whom—is specified—
> Not murmur—not endearment—
> But simply—we obeyed—
> Obeyed—a Lure—a Longing?

> Oh Nature—none of this—
> To Law—said sweet Thermopylae
> I give my dying Kiss—
>   *(as printed in Trilling, including em-dashes; Fr 1584, circa 1882)*

Perhaps the poem's direct reference to classical Greece amplified its value for Trilling, given the tacit theory of world literature behind his anthology's selections of drama and fiction (for what Trilling considered "obvious reasons," the poems "are all English and American"). One matter, though, worried him. Acknowledging that "One of the tenets of modern literary criticism is that a poem is a self-contained entity" to which "knowledge of the personal life of the poet ... is considered irrelevant," he nevertheless conceded that for the purposes of this "striking little poem, there is at least one personal fact about the author which it is essential we bring to our reading – that the poet is a woman." (Indeed, she was the only woman whose poetry Trilling judged worthy of explication in *The Experience of Literature*, although Marianne Moore made it into the anthology's selection of supplemental readings.) "If we were not aware of this," Trilling added, "we might well be made uncomfortable by the poem, for its tone and diction seem appropriate to a woman but not to a man, and we would surely be ill at ease if we thought a man had been the writer. The poem is, as it were, based on the femininity of the poet."[1]

Jarring as some of its terms are today, Trilling's reading of 1967 was also prescient. At a distance of half a century, it takes very little interpretive pressure to turn his feminine Dickinson toward an outright feminist reading of her self-conscious intervention in the high male literary canon. Musing over the opening of the Greek poet Simonides' famous epitaph for the Spartans who fought to their death at the battle of Thermopylae – "Go tell the Spartans, thou who passest by / That here, obedient to their laws, we lie"[2] – Dickinson reads first for what the masculine martial ethos might be thought to repress: the "murmur" of protest, a word of "endearment" to a beloved left behind. Finding no purchase for these human, perhaps indicatively feminine, ties and emotions, she queries the epitaph further for evidence of a more difficult kind of desire that could motivate so extreme a renunciation: a deathly "Longing" for some "Lure" lost or forever over the horizon. ("We do not think enough of the Dead as exhilirants," Dickinson wrote elsewhere, in a late prose fragment: "– they are not dissuaders but Lures –" [PF 50, *Letters* III: 919].) Framing her question to Simonides' epitaph as one of desire brings the dead letter of the Greek inscription to life – it talks back to her – and turns Dickinson into the arbiter of an internal dialogue between traditionally gendered personifications or principles, Nature and Thermopylae, the goddess and the hero. The hero rejects Nature's hypothesis that desire motivated the Spartan warriors' self-sacrifice, asserting instead that they died for "Law" – for culture, as it were, rather than for nature. Although "rebuked," as Trilling puts it, "the feminine voice is not to be silenced"; it returns "in the peculiarly feminine epithet by which it characterizes the great event" as "sweet Thermopylae." When the Spartan warriors consent to describe their final salute to Law as a kiss, says Trilling, "they have been beguiled into taking the feminine view of their actions, and Law and Love are made one."[3]

Trilling's 1967 reading of Dickinson's poem ends here, and he did not live to see the day in May 1989 when a group of students unfurled a banner over Columbia's Butler Library that added Dickinson's name, along with those of Sappho, Marie de France, Christine de Pizan, Sor Juana Ines de la Cruz, Brontë, and Woolf, to the list of male sages – Homer, Sophocles and Plato, Cicero and Vergil – engraved along the library's entabulature. (A photograph of the banner became a famous image of the "canon wars" in American literary scholarship of the 1980s and 1990s.[4]) By 1989, many feminist readers of Dickinson, myself among them, would be deeply unsatisfied with her lonely placement in Trilling's anthology, as if one writer could represent the literary potential of half the human race, and unsatisfied as well with the easy reconciliation Trilling pronounces to the conflict between feminine and masculine principles in Dickinson's poem. Not that Trilling's little essay on Dickinson dwells on the connotations of masculinity; for him, masculinity is the "unmarked" term (using the distinction that feminist criticism imported from linguistics), the universal norm against which femininity stands out as a "peculiar" deviation that must account for itself. As Trilling himself explains, "The word femininity is never used in a neutral sense but always with the intention of praise; it connotes charm, delicacy, tenderness."[5] All these aspects of Trilling's interpretation and more would become subject to feminist critique. Yet on one point Trilling and subsequent feminist readers of Dickinson, perhaps even most readers of Dickinson today, would agree: admitting knowledge of Dickinson's biographical identity as a woman writer is important, perhaps even essential, to appreciating her literary value.

Picking up the threads of Trilling's reading of "Go tell it" in the present day, it seems all the more important to bring masculinity into focus alongside femininity, and to resist collapsing these terms too readily onto actual women and men. Dickinson herself, the biographical woman writer, produces both the masculine and the feminine poles of her poem. Notably, the first four lines of "Go tell it" use no diction marked as feminine and deploy a verbal economy close to that of Simonides' epitaph itself. Concision or terseness, as an attribute of style, is often typed as masculine, prolixity (not always with the intention of praise) as feminine: the man of few words versus the chattering woman. Dickinson's truncated invocation of Simonides' famously compressed epigraph both invokes this typing and lays her own implicit claim to a masculine terseness of style. (A reader interested in the visual styles of Dickinson's writing may also appreciate once again how the "bolder and more abrupt" character of her late handwriting, as Mabel Loomis Todd described it, differs in this manuscript from "the delicate, running hand" expected "of our elder gentlewomen."[6]) When the poem then divides into feminine and masculine voices, it suggests that femininity – if not quite only a mask or a masquerade, as feminist critics have sometimes considered it – is but one mode among other styles available to Dickinson.[7] From the perspective of present-day feminist criticism, we might amend Trilling's conclusion that this poem is "based on the femininity of the poet" to say rather that "Go tell it –" is based on Dickinson's access to both masculinity and femininity as vocabularies for desire and differentiation.

From this present-day critical perspective, masculinity in "Go tell it –" looks more complicated as well. Although the poem's voice of "Thermopylae" ascribes the Spartans' motivation to obedience rather than desire, Dickinson was familiar with a range of literary works, both Victorian and ancient, in which "Longing" is very much a masculine trait. The classical Greek term for the kind of melancholy desire invoked by Dickinson's "Longing" is *pothos*, as the Greek lexicons at Amherst Academy could have told Dickinson, and it is attached at key moments in the epic tradition to men. Pothos, as Gregory Nagy observes, is the longing that Achilles feels for dead Patrocles (*Iliad* XIX.321) as well as the longing that, Achilles foretells, the desperate Greek forces will feel when Achilles withdraws from them (*Iliad* I:240) and will feel still more when he dies.[8] The pothos of Odysseus urges him home to his wife, and pothos drives him out to sea once again; Dickinson certainly knew Tennyson's great poem of that longing, "Ulysses." Associated "with mourning and bereavement," according to Tim Whitmarsh, pothos has also "a more general association with destruction, for its subject as well as its object. It is a destabilising emotion, which can also portend tragedy for the desirer."[9] Longing can send men to war, as Dickinson's poem imagines; or as it does in Thucydides, where "a *pothos* for distant spectacles and sights motivates the young to support the disastrous Sicilian expedition," or as in the life of Alexander the Great, where "a *pothos* for conquest and exploration" drives him to Asia.[10] By the time Dickinson wrote "Go tell it –," the longing of Greek pothos was also coming to be associated, in some Anglophone literary circles, with the social impossibility of homoerotic passion, "Greek love." For those nineteenth-century women writers who aspired to the classical learning traditionally reserved for elite men's education, Yopie Prins speculates, Greek literature offered a particularly privileged site for the "vicarious experience of pathos," a grafting of their own longing for distant horizons onto the pothos of classical Greek letters that allowed women to test "the imaginative possibilities of [their] homoerotic projections and sympathetic identifications" with masculine forms of yearning[11] – possibilities such as the "dying kiss" that Dickinson's poem projects onto the Spartans.

"Go tell it –" taps into the "Lure" that Greek held for many nineteenth-century Anglophone women writers, but from a certain critical distance. Unlike some women of her time and circumstances, Dickinson did not aspire to a classical higher education, although she extravagantly admired women writers among her contemporaries, especially Elizabeth Barrett Browning and George Eliot, whose classical learning rivaled that of Oxbridge-educated men. Dickinson's classical allusions (along with many other of her literary allusions) are often reduced to the bare nubbin of a proper name: Thermopylae, Jason ("Finding is the first Act," Fr 910), Prometheus ("The smouldering embers blush –," Fr 1143). Notably, Jason turns out to be a "sham"; and the manuscript of "The smouldering embers blush –" shows that Dickinson experimented with writing the name of Prometheus out of that poem. It seems that Dickinson strongly preferred not to idealize the glamorous otherness of Greek letters or to allow her poems to depend on classical decor or overt displays of learning. What Dickinson does, however, share with her Greekling contemporaries such as Barrett Browning, in a poem such as "Go tell it –," is their fundamental intuition that the emergence of the woman of letters is bound up with the longings of men and may express itself through sympathetic identification with, or projection into, male-authored literary traditions.

Dickinson's editors date "Go tell it –" to about 1882, and the likely biographical surround of the poem is also revealing about Dickinson's relationship to male longing and male letters. She received word in April 1882 of the death of the Reverend Charles Wadsworth, a revered preacher whose services Dickinson probably attended during her 1855 stay in Philadelphia and with whom she maintained a relationship punctuated by two visits from him, in 1860 and 1880; although none of her letters to him and only one from him to her survives, many readers have identified Wadsworth with the "Master" of Dickinson's anguished writings from the late 1850s and early 1860s. On April 27, 1882 Ralph Waldo Emerson died. In April 1882 Judge Otis Phillips Lord was presiding over a locally celebrated murder trial in Springfield, Massachusetts, that Dickinson was following closely in the *Springfield Republican*. On April 30, 1882

Dickinson began a letter to Lord that took on greater urgency when word reached Amherst that Lord was seriously ill. Even before learning of Lord's collapse, she was preoccupied with the death of heroes:

> I am told it is only a pair of Sundays since you went from me. I feel it many years. Today is April's last—it has been an April of meaning to me. I have been in your Bosom. My Philadelphia has passed from Earth, and the Ralph Waldo Emerson – whose name my Father's Law Student taught me, has touched the secret Spring. Which Earth are we in? (April 30, 1882, *Letters* 750)

Dickinson's chain of associations links her dutiful Lord, absent on the Law's business, with Charles Wadsworth ("My Philadelphia"); with Benjamin Newton, who talked literature with Dickinson while reading law in her father's office, and who died young; and with Ralph Waldo Emerson. Whatever any of these men may have been to her in life, in this late letter none enjoys a singular status as Master. They are recruited instead into Dickinson's personal pantheon, her nobility of the word rather than the sword. Plato, Vergil, Cicero; Wadsworth, Emerson, Lord: Dickinson's tribute to her men of letters elevates them, certainly, while at the same time demonstrating her own power to canonize heroes.

This letter is well known as a document of Dickinson's attachment to Lord, testimony both to its strength and to where she drew its limits: "I have a strong surmise that moments we have *not* known are tenderest to you. Of their afflicting Sweetness, you only are the judge." Dickinson's self-consciously literary letter shares with "Go tell it –" a ruling theme of heroic masculine self-sacrifice and dedication to law (underlined in her punning on Judge Lord's vocation) over personal desire. Both letter and poem refer to their male heroes metonymically, identifying them with the geographical seat of their power or fame – Thermopylae, "My Philadelphia" – as Dickinson also liked to refer to Lord as her "sweet Salem" and to herself as "his Amherst" (*Letters* 751). Her titles imply parity, a meeting of law and literature as rival noble powers connected by this likeness even as they are distinguished by gender. Dickinson's "strong surmise" about the extent of Lord's longing for her evokes or personifies conventional femininity (Trilling's "tenderness" and "delicacy") as a kind of third entity appearing in the generative space she maintained between "Amherst" and "Salem": an imaginative projection of "afflicting Sweetness," not a simple lie but nevertheless a creative fiction that the lawyer in Lord might not own but that Dickinson the writer has induced in him. When Dickinson in her turn personifies "Tenderness" in the space between them, it becomes a more masculine power: "Tenderness has not a Date – it comes – and overwhelms" (*Letters* 750). These longing projections of masculinity and femininity are not identical to the beloved other in his or her entirety. Lord "still has many closets that Love has never ransacked," Dickinson reminds him, a gracious way of warning Lord that neither will she ever be fully open to him.

Like "Go tell it –," Dickinson's letter to Lord (which may never have been sent[12]) is both an italicized performance of femininity and a loving reading of masculinity. The poem's "sweet Thermopylae" may well owe something to Dickinson's biographical suspense and concern for her dutiful "sweet Salem," as well as to her enjoyment of ventriloquizing his yearning for her from a manageable distance. "The Mind lives on the Heart / Like any Parasite," she had written a few years earlier (Fr 1384E, as sent to Higginson in 1876), suggesting that Dickinson's own theory of poetry was not so stringent as some twentieth-century criticism would be in separating the emotional life of the biographical author from the literary work. The poem, however, speaks of the closets in Dickinson's life that Lord's love never ransacked: her poetry and her enduring sense of vocation. Dickinson's poem, by contrast with the letter, is impersonal; in this way, it is like the majestic Law to which the Spartans pledge their deaths. Grafting her own revisionist intention into Simonides' famous epitaph, Dickinson makes it bear a different message both backward and forward in time. "Ought Women to Learn the Alphabet?" her "Preceptor" Higginson had asked, in an essay of that title published in *The Atlantic Monthly* in 1859: "There the whole question lies. Concede this little fulcrum, and Archimedes will move the world before she has done with it: it becomes a mere question of time."[13] The news from Thermopylae is that a woman has learned the alphabet.

One of the foundational insights of feminist literary criticism is that a poem need not be conventionally feminine – charming, delicate, and tender, to recall Trilling's definition once more – in order to be premised on its author's recourse to the vocabulary of masculinity and femininity (in shorthand, on the system of relationships that social science calls "gender"), or at one more remove, on the author's bio-graphical identity as a woman. A poem that desecrates or dissents from the prevailing conventions of femininity also, inevitably, depends on those conventions for its intelligibility. Such poems can of course be written by male authors: a famous example is Shakespeare's Sonnet 130, "My mistress' eyes are nothing like the sun," which boasts of the poet's love for a woman who is neither a "goddess" nor conventionally beautiful. Shakespeare's sonnet offers its informed readers both a sense of superiority to the poetic clichés being mocked (the spun-gold hair and coral lips of the Petrarchan sonnet) and access to a countervailing aesthetic that prizes dark, indelicate female forms. The sonnet self-consciously demonstrates that new kinds of literary value emerge in part by creative destruction, through the desecration of too-familiar idols and the aggressive desub-limation of figurative languages so dead through overuse as to have lost their purchase in the world of flesh and blood. And although the relationship between new kinds of literary value and new human possibilities may never be one-way, immediate, or predictable – critics of Shakespeare's sonnets famously differ over whether Sonnet 130's satire on conventional representations of feminine beauty is itself tinged with misogyny – we cannot value literature very highly if we do not think it real.

Feminist literary criticism particularly prizes the kinds of lit-erary value and the addition to human possibilities generated when a woman, writing in the person of a woman, creatively desecrates the conventions of femininity. "If snow be white, why then her breasts are dun; / If hairs be wires, black wires grow on her head," Shakespeare writes of his mistress, outraging poetic convention but not the expec-tation of his time that men typically represent women rather than the other way around. Something different – not for that simple reason superior, but nevertheless a different addition to literary and human possibility – enters the world when Dickinson dares her reader to

> Rearrange a "Wife's" Affection!
> When they dislocate my Brain!
> Amputate my freckled Bosom!
> Make me bearded like a man!   (*Fr 267A*, *ll. 1–4*)

This poem, no less than "Go tell it –, " is "based on the femininity of the poet," to quote Trilling once again, but to scarifying effect. It is one thing for poetry to re-value an aesthetically denigrated female body – its dun or freckled breasts, its unruly hair. It is another thing when that female body speaks for its own desires and when the poetic convention of the blazon, the itemization of feminine body parts, begins with the brain; an optimistic version of Dickinson's poem might have found a way of stopping here. This poem, however, suspends the desiring female body between equal twin horrors of exposure and invisibility. Unlike the coral lips and snowy breasts of the conventional blazon, and unlike their counterparts in the counter-aesthetic of Shakespeare's sonnet, Dickinson's parts cannot become visible, cannot be *read* and still remain feminine, or even integral as a body. Nor – as I argued of this poem in the previous chapter – does the speaker's nightly assumption of her queenly "diadem" mitigate the daily torture of reproducing her own invisibility. Where "Go tell it –" bears an optimistic message about the woman poet's capacity to identify with or project herself into a male-authored high literary tradition, "Rearrange a 'Wife's Affection" projects a dire outcome for the encounter of Petrarchan poetic convention with female flesh, blood, and brain. The subjects and objects of language and desire will not change places in this tradition without forcing.

No poem by Dickinson about this forcing is more famous than the following lines, which the late poet Adrienne Rich (invoking the dedication to the first printing of Shakespeare's sonnets) called "the real 'onlie begetter'"[14] of her immensely influential feminist interpretation of Dickinson's life and work:

My Life had stood – a Loaded Gun –
In Corners – till a Day
The Owner passed – identified –
And carried Me away –

And now We roam in Sovreign Woods –
And now We hunt the Doe –
And every time I speak for Him
The Mountains straight reply –

And do I smile, such cordial light
Opon the Valley glow –
It is as a Vesuvian face
Had let it's pleasure through –

And when at Night – Our good Day done –
I guard My Master's Head –
'Tis better than the Eider Duck's
Deep Pillow – to have shared –

To foe of His – I'm deadly foe –
None stir the second time –
On whom I lay a Yellow Eye –
Or an emphatic Thumb –

Though I than He – may longer live
He longer must – than I –
For I have but the power to kill,
Without – the power to die –   (Fr 764A, circa 1863)

Rich's 1975 essay "Vesuvius at Home: The Power of Emily Dickinson," followed a decade later by Susan Howe's book-length meditation, *My Emily Dickinson*, also organized around this poem, together made "My Life had stood – a Loaded Gun – " not only a poet's poem but also a central, all but inevitable touchstone for feminist valuations of Dickinson's writing.

Like the famous optical illusion that can be seen alternately as a vase or two opposing faces, this poem reads as a tale either of exultant liberation or of the most profound subjugation. For its narrator, the reward of being seen, "identified," is the freedom of the woods; the powers of speech and the exercise of force, even deadly force; and mutual recognition, exchanged with the Owner/Master on a titanic scale. At the most abstract level, the poem plots the metamorphosis of an object into a speaking subject: a socially resonant plot of liberation, in Dickinson's mid-nineteenth-century Atlantic world and beyond, not only for women but for also for enslaved Africans and other aspirants to full political and civil agency. And yet the poem is also premised on the reverse, the transformation of a human subject, a Life, into an object, the gun. Moreover, a price is paid for this liberating metamorphosis in the poem: paid first of all by the hunted Doe and the pillaged Eider Duck whose down (plucked from her own breast to line her eggs' nest) plumps the Master's Deep Pillow; and paid at last by the gun itself, which like other protagonists in myth and legend who ask for and are granted immortal life, finds that the devil is in the details: "For I have but the power to kill, / Without – the power to die –." From the perspective of the Doe or the Eider Duck, the gun is no liberator. Femininity is marked in this poem, not just linguistically but as a target is marked, and the gun cannot choose but to be its marker. Even from the gun's perspective, as Susan Howe observes, "Liberty looks like banishment," and "[f]reedom to explore ... may be linked forever to loneliness, exile and murder": "She the man-made Gun; Poet influenced by the work of many men, tied by a cord of attachment to her Master," roams the Sovereign wood cut off from any human community, especially any community that could include other women as speaking subjects. In Howe's summary, "[t]his is a tragic poem. A pioneer's terse epic."[15]

Adrienne Rich, drawn to the same elements of Dickinson's poem that lure Howe, sees in it an "ambivalence toward power" endemic to the condition of the woman poet, for whom "[t]he union of gun with hunter embodies the danger of identifying and taking and taking hold of her forces, not least that in so doing she risks defining herself – and being defined – as aggressive, as unwomanly ... and as potentially lethal."[16] Under Rich's description, however, the ambivalence driving "My Life had stood –" is susceptible to amelioration, if not in the poem itself (where the last stanza offers "no resolution, only a further extension of ambivalence"[17]) then in the long run of human history. What is "defined" in one way could be redefined in another; the problem is partly or wholly one of social labeling. By imaging so forcefully the impulses and interdictions under which the woman poet writes, Dickinson may ultimately change them, lending her poem's aesthetic assault on the conventions of femininity, as Rich hopes, to a wholesale cultural relabeling of women's exercise of power. A poem "about possession by the daemon, about the dangers and risks of such possession if you are a woman, about the knowledge that power in a woman can seem destructive, and that you cannot live without the daemon once it has possessed you" points to a countervailing human and aesthetic ideal of self-possession, in which the woman poet (on behalf of all women) is fully capable of "identifying and taking and taking hold of *her* forces."[18]

Oh Nature – none of this – replies Susan Howe. To Howe's mind, the powers summoned in "My Life had stood – a Loaded Gun –" really are, and ever were, lethal. Power doesn't just *seem* destructive, it *is* destructive, among its other attributes; ask Nat Turner or King Lear or the Wampanoag. "All power ... is utterly unstable" for Howe as well, too much so to sustain Rich's dream of the self-possessed female subject – Eve replacing Adam in the woods of a prelapsarian Eden, in guiltless enjoyment of sovereignty.[19] From the title of her study forward, Howe implicitly endorses Rich's thesis that Dickinson's poem is all about power and possession. But Howe actively values Dickinson's unstable possession by and of other writers and works, especially but not only male voices and male-authored works: Robert Browning's Childe Roland, Shakespeare, James Fenimore Cooper's Leatherstocking, Jonathan Edwards. The forces running through poetry, Howe asserts, cannot be owned by any one person, and the goal of poetry therefore cannot be self-possession: instead, "Poetry leads past possession of self to transfiguration beyond gender."[20] The plots of liberation are not altogether dead in Howe's reading of Dickinson, but they are changed: "This acutest lyric poet . . . sings of liberation into an order beyond gender."[21]

Did Dickinson aspire to "transfiguration beyond gender" as a human or aesthetic possibility? The evidence of her poems, even this one, seems mixed. The genderless gun of "My Life had stood –" is trapped in service to a rigorously gendered order, with no evident possibility of escape from a kind of bad aesthetic eternity: figured, certainly, but without the trans.[22] Elsewhere, however, Dickinson's demand of God and her readers that we "Behold the Atom I preferred – / To all the lists of clay!" ("Of all the Souls that stand create –," Fr 279) exults in the power to strip the Atom of any and every social attribute it bore in life, including gender. When "Sense from spirit – files away –" in this poem, the order it leaves behind does indeed seem transfigured beyond gender, although not – importantly – beyond the will and capacity to possess. Dickinson's experiment with giving linguistic form to a genderless afterlife must, of course, steer clear of the gendered personal pronouns and gender-marked nouns of "My Life had stood –," but this poem's stylistic virtuosity goes deeper. Where "My Life had stood" is studded with memorable concrete nouns – the gun itself, the Owner, the Master, the Eider Duck stalked by Yellow Eye and emphatic Thumb – "Of all the Souls that stand create" is a poem carried primarily by its verbs. The speaker's active verbs – "I elected" and "I preferred" – frame the poem at beginning and end. They confront the poem's two passive verbs, "this brief Tragedy of Flesh – / *Is shifted*, like a Sand … / And Mists – *are carved* away," the elided agent of which is presumably God, while the subjects of these passive verbs are mass nouns (nouns that have no plural form in common grammatical usage because they name an undifferentiated mass), or nearly so: Flesh, Sand, Mists – and, later in the poem, clay. Dickinson's grammatically unorthodox "a Sand" underscores the carving away of individual identity from every noun in the poem. Between the speaker's active *I* and God's agentless actions stand several highly abstract nouns and noun phrases linked for the most part by verbs of stasis: "Sense," "spirit," "Subterfuge," "that which is," "that which was," "Figures" and "Front," leading up to the most abstract noun of all, the object of Dickinson's election, the Atom. In the liberating and entrapping narrative of "My Life had stood – a Loaded Gun –," a human subject (a Life) becomes an object (a gun) that becomes a subject (a destructive agent), suspended between the slain Doe and the sleeping Master, that can't become human again. The narrative grammar of this poem is much simpler: an absolute subject possesses an absolute object. The markedly different linguistic resources summoned in "Of all the Souls that stand create –" by contrast with "My Life had stood –" underline the aesthetic force and inventiveness required to write beyond gender.

Dickinson was not the only nineteenth-century woman writer to imagine gender's afterlife through the Last Judgment. "I am not talking to you now through the medium of custom, conventionalities, nor even of mortal flesh: it is my spirit that addresses your spirit; just as if both had passed through the grave, and we stood at God's feet, equal – as we are!" Jane Eyre hurls these famous words at her beloved employer Mr. Rochester, in a novel that Dickinson found "electric" (*Jane Eyre*, chapter 23; *Letters* 811). Christianity's master narrative of death, resurrection, and judgment afforded both Charlotte Brontë and Dickinson (as it did John Milton before them) license to speculate about what "transfiguration beyond gender" might conceivably look like. If believers, "in the resurrection[,] . . . neither marry nor are given in marriage but are like angels in heaven" (Matthew 22:30 KJV), do their resurrected bodies leave gender behind? Or only the inequality of gender as lived in the bodies they hitherto knew?

Unlike Dickinson's poem, Charlotte Brontë's realistic novel must return its heavenly ideal of equality to the world of mortal clay. Male flesh pays a famously dire price for spiritual equality in *Jane Eyre*: blinded, scarred, and with one hand amputated, Rochester survives the fire that kills his mad wife to marry Jane and live happily ever after. "I was then his vision," says Jane in the novel's closing chapter, and she remains "still his right hand" even after Rochester regains some sight; no other woman, she claims, can ever have been so completely married to her husband, so "absolutely bone of his bone and flesh of his flesh" (*Jane Eyre*, chapter 38). Legions of readers in Brontë's time and afterward have debated this ending, and Elizabeth Barrett Browning paid homage to it in her novel-poem *Aurora Leigh*, another of Dickinson's "electric" books, which also ends with a union

between the narrator and her blinded lover. Dickinson reduces
Brontë's and Barrett Browning's romantic plots to their bare, abstract
essence in "Of all the Souls that stand create –." Working outside of
realistic narrative, Dickinson can delete the agents of her poem's
passive verbs and abstract the implicit violence that carves and files
her Atom down to size. Bodies fall away in Dickinson's poem along
with all the other material surround of the novelistic romance plot,
but the syntax of power remains: the poem's "I" has agency, the
poem's Atom does not. Whether a reader sees Dickinson's poem as
beyond gender or as gender's apotheosis may depend on whether she
thinks of gender as a noun (like a gun or a Doe) or as a verb, an action
that positions subjects in relation to objects. Either way, there can be
no doubt of how radical a transformation Dickinson works on the
cultural materials of femininity and masculinity.

"That Mrs. Browning fainted, we need not read *Aurora Leigh* to
know, when she lived with her English aunt; and George Sand
'must make no noise in her grandmother's bedroom.' Poor children!
Women, now, queens, now! And one in the Eden of God" (*Letters* 234).
Dickinson's letter to her Norcross cousins marking the death in 1861
of Elizabeth Barrett Browning is much cited today as evidence of her
lively interest in women writers as a group. She was by no means alone
in this interest. The emergence of women writers en masse into the
nineteenth-century literary marketplace was a historical phenomenon widely acknowledged on both sides of the Atlantic, by men as
well as women; by supporters such as Thomas Wentworth Higginson
and by detractors such as Nathaniel Hawthorne, whose private denun-
ciation of the "damn'd mob of scribbling women" registered their
invasion with alarm. Dickinson read women writers of power avidly
but cultivated some distance, as Betsy Erkkila observes, from the most
conventionally feminine work of her American contemporaries.[23]
Even Barrett Browning and Sand did not set Dickinson an example of
unconstrained possibility; in them too Dickinson "recognized the
long sufferance of women writers split between their sense of possibility of creative and queen-like power and the actual limits of their
lives as women."[24]

"Arrogant, I think I have written lines which qualify me to be The Poetess of American ... Who rivals? Well, in history Sappho, Elizabeth Barrett Browning, Christina Rossetti, Amy Lowell, Emily Dickinson, Edna St. Vincent Millay—all dead." Sylvia Plath's journal entry of 1958, now almost as well-known as Dickinson's letter, underlines how rapidly Dickinson was recruited into the twentieth century's emergent canon of women writers with the posthumous publication of her poetry. Like Adrienne Rich (whom Plath acknowledged in this same journal entry as her nearest rival) and Susan Howe – and, for that matter, like Dickinson herself – Plath came to her poetic vocation in a literary world in which women writers constituted a meaningful category, for better and worse a marked group. By the 1950s, Dickinson was an established figure in that literary landscape. Plath's mother, under the tutelage of an enthusiastic English teacher, had taken Emily Dickinson as her "new bible" in high school; Sylvia wrote home from Smith College in 1953 to send her mother two poems, of which she remarked that "any resemblance to Emily Dickinson is purely intentional."[25] As her role in the Plath family correspondence underlines, Dickinson had already become a canonical presence for aspiring women writers – both an icon of possibility and a resource for stylistic and thematic invention – several decades before that small group of Columbia students unfurled their banner claiming for her this place in literary history.

Plath's direct imitations of Dickinson were terrible, sententious and repetitive, but the interchange between her accomplished later work and Dickinson's poetry seems more equal even if, for that very reason, its identification must be more tentative. "Mushrooms," included in Plath's first collection, *The Colossus* (1960), takes up where Dickinson's "The Mushroom is the Elf of Plants –" leaves off. Where Dickinson's mushroom is a fleeting nineteenth-century confidence man, here one moment and gone the next, Plath's mushrooms are the "Bland-mannered" spawn of mid-twentieth-century American organizational culture, speaking in the collective first-person plural, "white" and "discreet," stereotypically feminine in "asking / little or nothing" for themselves and "Diet[ing] on water," but nevertheless on their way to "Inherit the earth. Our foot's in the door."[26] Where

Dickinson's poem is composed in regular iambic feet, each line ending in a strong stress, the predominant metrical foot of Plath's freer poem shifts back and forth between trochees (an accented followed by an unaccented syllable) and dactyls (an accented syllable followed by two unaccented syllables), with most of the lines ending in weak stresses – a "distinctive falling rhythm" that Helen Vendler identifies as the metrical signature of Plath's emergence as a poet,[27] a "feminine" rhyme pattern it would be called if Plath's poem were more regularly rhymed rather than off-rhymed, as Dickinson's rhyme would be called "masculine." Plath's closing line, suggesting that her put-upon mushrooms have learned something from the repertory of the door-to-door salesman, brings her poem once again back to Dickinson's agile trickster mushroom, highlighting Plath's implicit claim on Dickinson's work: her foot is inside Dickinson's door.

Both Dickinson's and Plath's mushroom poems accord aesthetic recognition to the overlooked, the despised, the unwanted, the out-of-place; but Plath's poem makes a direct claim for the collective powers of the weak in ways that Dickinson's does not. Soft, blind, colorless, voiceless, her mushrooms have no advantage except their numbers and their persistence, but they will inherit the earth that Dickinson's isolate mushroom is content to tarry on. The weak are neither attractive nor heroic, in Plath's representation, only relentless. Small wonder that Plath's "Mushrooms" is sometimes read and taught today (inaccurately, I think) as a poem of feminist insurgence. "Women in numbers have always disturbed me," Plath confessed to her journal at Smith,[28] with a buried pun on the ancient association between poetry and numbers; the emergence of women en masse into anyone's field, including the field of poetry, repels Plath at least as much as it fascinates her. (Similarly, Plath's famous series of poems about bees and bee-keeping circle around the humming hive, in contrast with Dickinson's typically tight focus on the individual; compare Plath's "The Arrival of the Bee Box" or "The Swarm" with Dickinson's bee as lone lover, or lone assailant, in Fr 134, "Did the Harebell loose her girdle," and Fr 1213, "Like Trains of Cars on Tracks of Plush.") If Plath's poem is more programmatic than Dickinson's, that is in part because for Plath, Dickinson's poems are always already there, demanding of her "Are you – Nobody – too?" (Fr 260). Plath's "Mushroom" replies to Dickinson by envisioning a crowd of no-bodies, an infinite number of zeros combining to make an irresistible force, in a deeply ambivalent parable of liberation.

Weakness and collective anonymity were not, however, Plath's only or inevitable poetic postures in relation to Dickinson's over-whelming example.[29] The famous opening lines of "Ariel," which became the title poem of Plath's second, posthumous collection – "Stasis in darkness / Then the substanceless blue / Pour of tor and distance" – recapitulate and reverse the opening of "My Life had stood – a Loaded Gun –."[30] Here Plath's speaker, even more abruptly than Dickinson's gun, is catapulted from dark corners into the free-dom of the open landscape. But where Dickinson's opening stanza is a grammatically complete compound sentence that assigns distinct roles to the Owner and the gun, Plath's opening lines consist only of noun phrases. "Ariel" begins not with a subject setting an object into motion, but with the impression of "substanceless" movement itself, "pure energy in motion" (in the words of Susan Van Dyne) and prior to matter; out of this formless energy precipitates a combined subject/object, Plath and her horse, "God's lioness" (in Hebrew, "Ariel" means "the Lion of God").[31] The poem's title allusion to Shakespeare suggests that Plath may be the master here, the wizard whose horse (named after the spirit in Shakespeare's *The Tempest*) does her bid-ding; but Plath also recalls Percy Bysshe Shelley's identification of the romantic poet with Ariel, the guardian servant-spirit "Imprisoned ... / In a body like a grave" ("With a Guitar, to Jane"). Who is the owner here, and who is owned? Who is the master, who the servant on this breakaway ride? Using every aesthetic resource at hand – grammar, imagery, literary allusion, meter – Plath's poem gallops to outrun the dichotomies of the domestic world and the gendered body.[32] Merged with the force that "Hauls me through air–," Plath "unpeel[s]" daily life's "dead stringencies" from her "White Godiva," distances herself from "The child's cry," and ultimately transfigures her life, like Dickinson's gun, into a weapon seeking out a Vesuvian face: an arrow flying "Suicidal, at one with the drive / Into the red / Eye, the cauldron of morning" (*Ariel* 27).

Dickinson's gun, though, never overtly turns on its Master. Whether Plath's arrow drives to kill the eye toward which it flies along with the *I* that flies; whether this drive can be other than lethal to its object and deadly for the poet herself; whether transfiguration beyond gender entails carving or peeling away the gendered body – are all open questions that Plath's poem poses both backward and forward in time: backward toward Dickinson's poetry, and forward – *Go tell it* – to readers who continue to value both Dickinson and Plath the more for the history of women's writing that connects them.

4 Her American materials

What part of Dickinson's value lies in her identity as an American writer? This question would not have seemed strange to Dickinson herself, nor to most of her English-speaking contemporaries on either side of the Atlantic. American literary culture in the years leading up to the Civil War was much preoccupied with asserting its independence of British models and British tutelage; the emergence of an original American literature, it was frequently argued, would ratify the political independence asserted by Great Britain's North American colonies in 1776, consolidated in the constitution of 1789, and defended in the war of 1812. The call for a new American literature was already old when Ralph Waldo Emerson, in his essay on "The Poet" (1844), lamented that

> We have yet had no genius in America, with tyrannous eye, which knew the value of our incomparable materials, and saw, in the barbarism and materialism of the times, another carnival of the same gods whose picture he so much admires in Homer; ... Yet America is poem in our eyes; its ample geography dazzles the imagination, and it will not wait long for metres.[1]

Around 1861, Dickinson copied out a poem that may be her most self-conscious contribution to the discourse of American literary nationalism – her most explicit attempt to assess the aesthetic value of her American materials. *Contra* Emerson, however, this poem starts from the premise that the distinctive value of those materials can only be known comparatively:

> The Robin's my Criterion for Tune –
> Because I grow – where Robins do –
> But, were I Cuckoo born –
> I'd swear by him –

The ode familiar – rules the Noon –
The Buttercup's my whim for Bloom –
Because, we're Orchard sprung –
But, were I Britain born,
I'd Daisies spurn –

None but the Nut – October fit –
Because – through dropping it,
The Seasons flit – I'm taught –
Without the Snow's Tableau
Winter, were lie – to me –
Because I see – New Englandly –
The Queen, discerns like me –
Provincially –   (*Fr 256A, Fascicle 11*)

Dickinson's initial metaphor presents her as the simple originary product of New England nature, a lyric bird "growing" and singing in her native landscape as naturally as "Robins do." From this starting point, however, the poem moves stealthily in the direction of cultural relativity and cultural hybridity, pointing to national differences that are constructed (through many kinds of effort) rather than simply read out of the natural landscape. Robins, after all, sing in England as well in Dickinson's Massachusetts, and buttercups grow in England as well; it is the long tradition of English poetry about the cuckoo that enables Dickinson to nominate the robin, in contrast and rivalry, as her emblem of American poetry. No less cultivated and cross-bred in her own way than New England's apple orchards, which sprung from European seeds, Dickinson's speaker has been "taught" the favored idioms of the English landscape through English literature: in William Wordsworth's "Nutting" and Jane Austen's *Persuasion* (to take two famous examples) it is the ripening of nuts, rather than New England's emblematic display of autumn leaves in color, that marks the close of the agricultural year.[2] The poem's increasingly cultivated and comparative perspective composes the American scene *as* a landscape, as an artistic "tableau," and finally as the emblem of a region, New England, whose name cannot escape reference to its mother country.

In this poem Dickinson's American eye, unlike Emerson's, is not vaunting and "tyrannous" in its new-found aesthetic authority but rather a cool leveler of privilege. Like the cat who may look at the queen in the ancient popular English proverb, Dickinson looks sideways at the Queen of England to discover someone "like" herself: like her in that the Queen too is rooted in a particular landscape and its distinctive register of sensory experience and literary tradition, while yet different from Dickinson in being perhaps less likely to grasp the situatedness of her own regal perspective. Dickinson's American gaze is no leveler of difference in and for itself; as Helen Vendler observes, Dickinson "prized distinction of species," and this poem implies that "a world without national differences would be boring."[3] Hers is instead a post-revolutionary world of plural aesthetic as well as political sovereignties, each equally relative to its surroundings – each equally "provincial" in a perspective that defers to no cultural metropole: not to London, not to Paris, nor even perhaps to Emerson's Boston.

The cat who looks at a queen may also turn her gaze on her own countrymen. And so Dickinson did, in the poem she copied out directly following "The Robin's my Criterion for Tune," on the reverse side of the same sheet of notepaper that she ultimately bound into Fascicle 11. Reversing her own previous claims on behalf of the American gaze in "The Robin's my Criterion for Tune," Dickinson presents in this poem a thoroughly undiscerning American eye:

I've known a Heaven, like a Tent –
To wrap it's shining Yards –
Pluck up it's stakes, and disappear –
Without the sound of Boards
Or Rip of Nail – Or Carpenter –
But just the miles of Stare –
That signalize a Show's Retreat –
In North America –

No Trace – no Figment – of the Thing
That dazzled, Yesterday,

No Ring – no Marvel –
Men, and Feats –
Dissolved as utterly-
As Bird's far Navigation
Discloses just a Hue –
A plash of Oars, a Gaiety –
Then swallowed up, of View.   (*Fr 257A, Fascicle 11*)

As if taking up Emerson's invitation to make American poetry out of America's carnivals, this poem begins with an extended simile comparing the departure of a mysterious "Heaven" to that of a one-ring circus folding up its tents to leave town. Dickinson marks the landscape and soundscape of this poem as quintessentially North American not only by registering the circus's profligate use of timber (a commercially valuable form of American material, one scarce and expensive back in the mother country) to bang up temporary structures for the purposes of pure popular amusement, but also by the hunger of its provincial audience, whose "miles of Stare" follow the departing performers long after the "Show's Retreat." In "The Robin's my Criterion for Tune," Dickinson's speaker is surely too cool to stare at the Queen; not so the spectacle-starved country crowd of this poem. Reducing this audience to their empty gaze, Dickinson evokes a small-town North America whose indiscriminate appetite for wonder is seldom slaked.

Like the beach-going public of Robert Frost's poem "Neither Out Far, Nor in Deep" (1936), who "All turn and look one way" at the ocean, this American stare seems vacant of objects or purpose – dazzled not, as Emerson would have it, by America's "ample geography" but by the gazers' own poverty of experience, which accepts a circus performance as representative of the world of "Men, and Feats –" beyond their own horizon. The phrase "miles of Stare" uses one of Dickinson's signature stylistic devices, that of taking plural or collective nouns and making them singular, as in her well-known line "I wish I were a Hay –" (Fr 379; Thomas Wentworth Higginson's editorial insistence on altering this line, for the 1890 *Poems*, to "I wish I were the hay" helped make it famous). But where "a Hay" violates grammatical convention by summoning an individual being out of a mass noun, in this poem the figure works in the other direction: agglomerating the Show's implied audience of individual men, women, and children into a single massed unit, Dickinson suggests that "Stare" may be one more gross American commodity, measured by the mile as lumber can be measured by the foot or hay by the ton. "Miles of Stare" does the same conceptual work as the familiar Latin motto on the Great Seal of the United States, adopted by the revolutionary Continental Congress in 1782, *E pluribus unum* – "Out of many, one" – and does it with just as much verbal economy, a preposition linking two nouns. In contrast with her nation's aspirational Latin, however, Dickinson's vernacular locution seems to imply her reservations about the mass or popular nature of her American materials.

If Dickinson's poem ended here, with what Michelle Kohler describes as "the blank stare of perplexed, abandoned viewers who expected the revelation of 'Heaven' but find only their own objectless vision,"[4] it might well read as an effort on Dickinson's part to assert her distance from and superiority to the American popular gaze and American mass culture. The simile of the poem's closing quatrain, however, turns away from looking critically *at* the American eye, to look once again *with* the American eye. Positioning herself once again with the avid spectators, eyes straining at the horizon, Dickinson follows a bird out of sight – a bird that she likens metaphorically to a boat, rowing and navigating the sky, even while the simile as a whole likens the vanishing bird to the departing circus, which in its turn was a figure for the heaven whose disappearance inaugurates the poem. As Michelle Kohler observes, this poem "unleashes a flurry of figures" in its effort to get at the "missing object" of the blank gaze, the revelation that never arrives[5]; by the poem's end, however, that revelation is no longer missed. Heaven, the nominal tenor of all the poem's metaphors, has been swallowed up by its figurative vehicles. Like her North American carnival, Dickinson's poem is content at last to be all show: in the end, Heaven is what we can see. This is not a poem focused on the agony of losing heaven, nor one in which Dickinson's "Business" is petitioning "the Cloud, / If any Power behind it, be, /

Not subject to Despair –" (Fr 292). There is no impulse here to stab, Ahab-like, through the "shining yards" of the circus tent to some more abstract revelation behind their dazzling appearances; the poem aligns itself instead with the craft that efficiently conjures gorgeous appearances out of mundane American materials – boards and canvas and nails – and with the popular American eye, not just willing but hungry to be dazzled. Like Henry David Thoreau in *Walden*, hoeing beans and following a night-hawk swooping and circling "like a mote in the eye, or in heaven's eye" (*Walden*, chapter 7), Dickinson's gaze fixes on an object in the sky's shining blankness, a solitary self-delighted movement, and finds it no less for losing it. Her vanishing bird is Dickinson's figure for a poetry capable of navigating with assurance between the mass American "Stare" and the dissolving North American sky.

For thirty-odd years following the appearance of Johnson's 1955 variorum edition of Dickinson's poems, it was more or less a critical given that elevating Dickinson into the company of Walt Whitman among American writers, with Emerson administering the rites and a cast of witnesses rotating among more distant figures such as Thoreau, Nathaniel Hawthorne, Jonathan Edwards, and Anne Bradstreet, was essential both for valuing Dickinson and for enlarging our sense of American literature as a whole. As the titles of landmark works along this path indicate – from Albert Gelpi's pairing of "Walt Whitman: The Self as Circumference" with "Emily Dickinson: The Self as Center" in *The Tenth Muse: The Psyche of the American Poet* (1975), to *Walt Whitman and Emily Dickinson: Poetry of the Central Consciousness* (1985) by Agnieszka Salska – criticism in this vein stressed the continuity of Dickinson's American literary inheritance from her Puritan ancestors through Emerson's secularized aesthetic version of the sovereign conscious I/eye, both master and creator of the American landscape it surveys.

In the waning years of the American Century, for very good reasons, it became much harder to value Dickinson by assimilating her poetry into a tradition of "American literature" conceived as a unitary, autonomous whole. Feminist criticism, as we saw in the previous chapter, began in the 1970s to explore Dickinson's affiliations with transnational communities of women writers; transatlantic criticism demonstrated how thoroughly entangled British and American literary cultures were in the nineteenth century; historicist criticism in the United States faced more squarely the national catastrophe of slavery and the Civil War; populist literary historians widened their focus from the Puritan New England lineage to culture outside the elites, looking *Beneath the American Renaissance* – in the title of David Reynolds' 1989 ambitious literary history – to locate what Reynolds' subtitle calls *The Subversive Imagination in the Age of Emerson and Melville.* Unnamed in Reynolds' title but centered on the jacket of *Beneath the American Renaissance* between photographs of Emerson and Melville, Dickinson looks out at readers in her authentic, unretouched daguerreotype image, identified by Reynolds with the American echoes of the great European revolutions of 1848.

National location and identity are by no means dead when we value Dickinson today, but these terms have taken on a more resolutely political cast, attuned to conflicts within the United States as well as between the United States and other nations. We are now likely to ask that a significant American poet not only look for the special revelation of God's presence in the American natural landscape, but also that she inquire into the varieties of human power exercised within that landscape, by whom and under what authority, and within what limitations. It seems increasingly important to recall that Dickinson grew up in a household intimate with the great political debates of her time. She saw her father elected to both houses of the Massachusetts state government in the 1830s and 1840s and to the U.S. House of Representatives in 1853; witnessed her father's ejection from national politics at the hands of the anti-immigrant, anti-Catholic "Know Nothing" Party revolt that swept Massachusetts in 1854; and visited Washington, D.C. in 1855 during the closing weeks of her father's term in office, as his beleaguered Whig party was crumbling underneath the weight of its compromises over slavery.[6] The profound structural conflicts of the mid-nineteenth-century United States – between the constitution's grounding in mass popular sovereignty and its guarantee of absolute individual rights, between direct and representative democracy, between equality and opportunity, between populism and elite-driven economic liberalism, between states' rights and national interests – ground and add gravity to Dickinson's poetic explorations of sovereignty and self-ownership, freedom and contract, delegation and consent, universalism and provincialism.

It is in the context of these defining tensions of American political life that Dickinson's self-consciously American poems assert her sovereign equality with the Queen of England and move toward and away from identifying with the popular American gaze. Looking for a critical language with which to place and appreciate the national antinomies structuring Dickinson's writing, Paul Crumbley suggestively calls her a "nonpopulist democrat."[7] Her poetry embodies these generative antinomies formally as well as thematically. Dickinson's typical four- and three-beat metrical lines take off from popular hymn and ballad forms rather than the many "high" meters and forms available to nineteenth-century Anglophone poetry – ranging from blank verse to sonnet forms to imitation of Greek hexameters – and yet she deploys her popular forms in ways that seem intended to strike discordantly on the popular ear. Both "The Robin's my Criterion for Tune" and "I've known a Heaven, like a Tent" play fast and loose with their underlying 4–3 quatrain template. The intermittent two-beat lines in the "The Robin's my Criterion for Tune" culminate in the poem's masterful closing two-beat epithet, "Provincially –"; rhymes are stretched out over lines ("Tune" and "noon") or compressed and repeated from line to line ("me," "New Englandly," "me," "Provincially") in ways that tug against the expectation of *abcb* quatrains. Every rhyme in "I've known a Heaven, like a Tent" is discordant until the final four lines, which settle into an *abcb* quatrain but tease Dickinson's reader to substitute in her own ear the conventional rhyme – missing to the eye – of "blue" for "Hue" and "View." Similarly, Dickinson's diction favors the colloquial middle registers of American English, hoarding multisyllabic Latinate words – such as "Provincially" – for emphasis, wrenching plain Germanic monosyllables into new grammatical places, as in "Miles of Stare," and eschewing the kinds of classical literary references and lumbering poetical

stage-sets that conventionally advertised nineteenth-century poets'
elite learning and demanded similar learning from their readers.
"What is commonest and cheapest and nearest and easiest is Me,"
Whitman proclaimed in his inaugural 1855 version of *Leaves of
Grass*.[8] Dickinson's liberties with poetic form and style assert in a
different aesthetic and political register her inalienable individual
right to craft discordance, difficulty, and rarity out of common
American materials.

For further examples of Dickinson writing as a "nonpopulist
democrat," consider another complementary pair of poems, "The
Props assist the House –" (Fr 729A) and "You've seen Balloons set –
Hav'nt You? (Fr 730), that Dickinson copied out onto a single sheet
of stationery around 1863 and ultimately bound into a fascicle
(Fascicle 35), as she previously did "The Robin's my Criterion for
Tune –" and "I've known a Heaven, like a Tent –." The first and
more familiar of these poems concerns individual rather than national
independence, likening the building of a house to the slow development of an autonomous "Soul":

> The Props assist the House –
> Until the House is built –
> And then the Props withdraw
> And adequate – Erect –
>
> The House support itself
> And cease to recollect
> The Scaffold and the Carpenter –
> Just such a Retrospect
> Hath the perfected Life –
> A Past of Plank – and Nail –
> And slowness – then the Stagings drop
> Affirming* it a Soul –   (Fr 729A)

The governing metaphor of the poem is homely or democratic enough,
evoking a typically American wood-framed house made without dis-
tinguishing ornament or luxury materials, a house "adequate"

without pretension, as the equivalent of the "perfected Life." It was during Dickinson's childhood that light-framed, nailed-lumber construction – "balloon framing," as it was called by the time Dickinson wrote this poem – became the most common building method for meeting America's ravenous demand for cheap, quickly constructed housing. In American national myth, and to some degree in national fact, anyone could aspire to build – or to become – this self-supporting house.

And yet Dickinson's metaphor in this poem is also, in Crumbley's terms, "nonpopulist" or even anti-populist. Having lived through her father's extensive renovations of the Homestead when the Dickinsons moved back into the family home in 1855, and his erection in 1856 of the elaborate Italianate, towered, and balconied Evergreens next door for Austin and Susan Dickinson, Emily Dickinson was well aware that simple American planks and nails could support complicated and by no means egalitarian social aspirations. Fulfilling the great American dream of individual self-sufficiency, her poem's House, once erected, forgets the common human community of labor that brought it into being. Is the same forgetfulness of its dependent origins to be expected of the perfected individual Soul?

By breaking off at the moment when the "Stagings" fall away from the accomplished Soul, Dickinson seems to suspend this question beyond her poem's ending. Hearing echoes of Christ and Calvary in the poem's Carpenter, planks, and nails, Helen Vendler believes that the "slow, repetitive work" of its painful spiritual education "is remembered by the perfected Soul in every detail, in every plank, in every nailing."[9] It's not clear to me, however, that Dickinson's poem provides this assurance, whether on a religious or a secular reading. Its emphasis on self-sufficiency stands apart from the central experience of American spiritual autobiography in the Protestant tradition, that of acknowledging the soul's utter dependence on God. The central concern of the poem is with the falling away of the perfected Soul's scaffolding rather than the pangs of its construction. Its mood and focus seem closer to Emerson's assertion, in "Experience" (1844), that "Souls never touch their objects": even in the death of his young son,

Emerson writes, "Something which I fancied was a part of me, which could not be torn away without tearing me, nor enlarged without enriching me, falls off from me, and leaves no scar. It was caducous."[10] That Dickinson sent a copy of this poem to Susan Dickinson, signed "Emily," only deepens the uncertainty of its tone: would Susan have received this as a message complimenting her own "perfected Life," rebuking her for withdrawing from their intimacy, asserting the poet's growing autonomy with respect to Susan's support – or as a completely impersonal lyric, addressed to everyone and no one? Any of these readings and all of them seem plausible. Both the words of the poem and Dickinson's sending it to Susan underline Dickinson's belief, as Elizabeth Hewitt puts it, that "the essential separation between persons is the very basis of social relations."[11] Like Emerson's essay, Dickinson's poem ties the American national dream of individual self-sufficiency to the perfected Soul's magnificent and terrible independence of its human objects.

   But then Dickinson once again turns over her manuscript page and reverses her perspective. The poem she copied out directly following "The Props assist the House" views a comparable ascent from the angle of those left behind on the ground. Here, as in "I've known a Heaven – Like a Tent," Dickinson looks both *at* and *with* the popular American gaze:

> You've seen Balloons set—Hav'nt You?
> So stately they ascend –
> It is as Swans – discarded You,
> For Duties Diamond –
>
> Their Liquid Feet go softly out
> Opon a Sea of Blonde –
> They spurn the Air, as 'twere too mean
> For Creatures so renowned –
>
> Their Ribbons just beyond the eye –
> They struggle – some – for Breath
> And yet the Crowd applaud, below –

They would not encore – Death –

The Gilded Creature strains – and spins –
Tips frantic in a Tree –
Tears open her imperial Veins –
And tumbles in the Sea –

The Crowd – retire with an Oath –
The Dust in Streets – go down –
And Clerks in Counting Rooms
Observe – "'Twas only a Balloon" –   (*Fr 730A, Fascicle 35*)

The apparently solid House that rises out of its scaffolding in the previous poem turns here into something much more unsubstantial, a gilded balloon, as if the circus tent of "I've known a Heaven – like a Tent" had split into its component parts of lumber and cloth. Where the erected House stands impassive as its supports fall away, this "Gilded Creature" actively spurns the air that invisibly supports her, as well as the human crowd of spectators assembled to watch her ascent. Unlike the House, however, this balloon, "strain[ing]" and "struggl[ing]" for buoyancy as she rises, is not remotely "adequate" to her own pretensions of self-sufficiency; her ribbons avail her nothing toward survival once she has ascended beyond the crowd's eye.

But then Dickinson's perspective shifts again, as the balloon's trailing skirts catch on a tree and she goes down, like Icarus, into the sea. The fall of the balloon becomes the fall of a spectacular and pathetic version of feminine social striving; the profane crowd that shrugs off the balloon's disaster is clearly coded as masculine and also as striving, albeit at a different class level and in vocational precincts restricted to men. Looking now *at* rather than *with* this vaguely threatening crowd, seeing as a nonpopulist democrat, Dickinson invites her readers to comprehend the balloon's vulnerable spectacle of femininity and the clerks' dusty, anonymous masculinity as mutually interdependent components of a single, but stratified and alienated, social order. The balloon's fatally excessive feminine trappings bring into higher relief the nominally gender-neutral self-sufficiency of the previous poem's "adequate – Erect" house, suggesting that this ideal may not be available to every American; it is a free and propertied white male aspiration, defined by its exclusions.

Dickinson's poem offers readers in miniature the kind of comprehensive social perspective more usually associated, by her time and in our own, with the realistic novel; or, in poetry, with Whitman's epic catalogs of American life. Dickinson renders the seriocomic social panorama that the lofty balloon could see, did she deign to look down – and were the balloon human, rather than a poetic figure, or a set of figures, humanized. We have seen the sun set, and read poems about it too; until buttonholed by Dickinson – "You've seen Balloons set—Hav'nt you?" – none of us may have seen the metaphor that Dickinson sees, nor thought to compare a sailing balloon to a swimming swan, all grace above and busily paddling invisible seas with invisible feet below, nor thought to identify a sinking balloon with that interesting character of so much great nineteenth-century fiction, the fallen woman. Dickinson's emphasis on the distancing mediation of figurative language distinguishes her social aesthetic from Whitman's vignettes of sympathetic identification. "I do not ask the wounded person how he feels. ... I myself become the wounded person," Whitman famously asserts, inviting us to enter the suffering of "the hounded slave" and "the mashed fireman with breastbone broken."[12] Dickinson's poem does not exactly invite readers to become the wounded balloon or the regal swan; they are too conspicuously figures to be persons in Whitman's sense. Nor does she, like Whitman, mediate between readers and the panorama in her own person, as a visible "I." Asking her readers to envision the swan's invisible feet and the balloon's disappearing ribbons (and assisting readers' interior vision with the props of sound: the propulsive consonant cluster *sp* in "spurn," the "Liquid" *l* picked up in "Blonde"), Dickinson's conspicuous figures instead call attention to the invisible labor required to produce their appearance of buoyant ease and self-sufficiency. And here, as Cristanne Miller suggests, the poem's concern for invisible labor implicates the human poet herself, the poem's absent "I," divided between the "magical gravityless ballet" of her figurative language and her daily household chores.[13] Both the balloon and Dickinson's poem ascend on viewless "feet" before falling back to earth.

From its vantage point in 1863, "You've seen Balloons set" looks both backward and forward in American popular culture: back to the "classic antebellum tale of seduction," as historian Karen Haltunnen summarizes it, in which a "raw but ambitious youth" – representative of the "unprecedented numbers of young men leaving their rural homes and families" for jobs in the counting-houses of America's rising cities – comes to grief in the city's "gorgeous theater" of confidence men and painted women; and forward to the increasingly "frantic panorama," as William Dean Howells called it, of post-Civil War American life, drawn to the sensational new pleasures of spectacular crashes, train wrecks and industrial mass disasters.[14] Where "The Props assist the House" imagines a "perfected" American selfhood that would presumably be more than "adequate" to resist the seductions of urban life and mass culture, perhaps even "adequate" to resist the pressures of time itself, "You've seen Balloons set" seems deliberately more open to its time and place. Along with "I've known a Heaven – like a Tent," "You've seen Balloons set" values America's gorgeous appearances over the impulse to stab through appearances in search of some firmer structure beyond them. We regret the ripping open of the Balloon's "Gilded" skin; a balloon torn is no revelation, but only a dead balloon. In this poem's final, haunting metaphor for seeing the invisible, the balloon bleeds out her "imperial Veins" into the atmosphere, writing her epitaph in air, on the air (recalling John Keats's famous deathbed epitaph for himself, "Here lies One whose Name was writ in Water"). Dickinson underscores the fragility or contingency of aesthetic work and its reception in the American scene. At the same time, she underscores the nature of aesthetic labor as effortful work, not less than the carpenter's; indeed, aesthetic labor may help hold the carpenter's work in memory. Dickinson's anti-populist, democratic aesthetic more often prefers to supplement, rather than discard, denigrate, or destroy, what the popular American eye can see.

The year 1863 has been called an *annus mirabilis* for Dickinson; her editor R. W. Franklin dates 295 poems to this single year, the highest total of any in her lifetime.[15] It was also the year of Gettysburg, the single most deadly battle of the bloodiest war in American history, and the year in which the fortunes of battle turned slowly but decisively to the Union armies – when it began to appear that Abraham Lincoln's famous prophecy of 1858, that "A house divided against itself cannot stand. ... I do not expect the Union to be *dissolved* – I do not expect the house to *fall* – but I *do* expect it will cease to be divided," might be fulfilled with the defeat of the South and the "ultimate extinction" of slavery in all the states.[16] It was the year in which the United States Congress and President Lincoln approved the first wartime conscription of men into military service in U.S. history, bringing the fighting closer to Austin Dickinson, who was of draft age; and the year in which Dickinson wrote to her mentor Thomas Wentworth Higginson, then commanding a black regiment of Union troops in South Carolina, that "War feels to me an oblique place" (*Letters* 280).[17]

How much does Dickinson's poetry of her most productive years (1861–1865) and afterwards owe by way of inspiration to the great national emergency of the Civil War? What does the connection between her writing and the war contribute to Dickinson's value to readers today? These are related but not identical questions, addressed to literary production and literary reception respectively. In the canon of American poetry at large there is no predictable relationship between Civil War subject matter and enduring literary reputation. Vast tracts of nineteenth-century American poetry directly inspired by the Civil War are now unread except by historical specialists. Herman Melville's *Battle-Pieces* (1866) remains in print and, in bits and pieces, in the standard pedagogical anthologies; Whitman's *Drum-Taps* (1865) reigns as the acknowledged poetic masterpiece of the war; but for every reader today who can place poems from Melville's and Whitman's great sequences, there are probably a dozen, in the U.S. and abroad, who can recall at least the first lines of Julia Ward Howe's "Battle Hymn of the Republic" (1862). Howe's poem leaves a reader in absolutely no doubt about its wartime subject matter and its author's allegiance to the Northern side of the conflict. The same cannot be said of many Dickinson poems of the Civil War years. If connecting them to the war adds to their value for readers – and increasing numbers of readers, both scholarly and popular, agree that it does – then in doing so we must also respect their frequently "oblique" relationship to the conflict.

On one end of a spectrum, "It feels a shame to be Alive –" (Fr 524), transcribed around early 1863, directly explores what Faith Barrett calls the "self-abasement" of the noncombatant "before the heroism of the soldiers who have sacrificed their lives."[18] The poem's central stanzas, as Barrett observes, allude to the North's economic straits in the depths of the war: by 1863 the growing strain of providing men and materiel to the front had prompted innovations in state financing – including an income tax and the introduction of "greenback" paper currency – as well as the introduction of conscription, throwing ever-greater heaps of lives as well as treasure into the conflict:

> The price is great – Sublimely paid –
> Do we deserve – a Thing –
> That lives – like Dollars – must be piled
> Before we may obtain?
>
> Are we that wait – sufficient worth –
> That such Enormous Pearl
> As life – dissolved be – for Us –
> In Battle's – horrid Bowl?   (Fr 524A, ll. 9–16)

These lines circle around Dickinson's characteristic preoccupation with the differing registers of individual, plural, and mass nouns or states of being – as in "a Hay" and "Miles of Stare" – but in what seems a deliberatively flat or abstract way: Liberty, the "Thing" that is the object of the war, is no more or less concrete a value than the piles of dollars and lives exchanged for it. The "Enormous Pearl" lost "In

Battle's – horrid Bowl" suggests both mass and individual life, but the distinction between the two is part of what dies when that pearl is "dissolved." The all but algebraic exchange of [lives + dollars] for "a Thing" – $x + y = z$ – is formally reversible; not so the dark entropy of the pearl, dissolved in the vintage that Julia Ward Howe saw trampled from the grapes of wrath.

This poem's implicit protest at the equivalence of lives and dollars would be tested a few months later when Austin Dickinson paid \$500 for a substitute to take his place in the Union army.[19] Although no record remains of what Emily Dickinson thought of her brother's decision not to fight, "It feels a shame to be Alive –" suggests that Dickinson would have claimed no moral standing from which to judge her brother. Here she can neither pledge her direct and fervent allegiance to the war's abstract cause, "Liberty," "a Thing" on which she only stands and waits, nor adopt a superior attitude of distance from the popular rhetoric honoring the sacrifice of "Men so brave" on behalf of that cause. She can only honor them and acknowledge, with horror and shame, her ineluctable part in the nation's collective pact of vicarious suffering – "pawn[ing] them "for Us" – a union from which she, like the dead soldiers, cannot secede and which she has no individual power to dissolve.

Another poem from later in 1863 returns once again to the registers of individual, plural, and mass death, to still more horrific effect. Reflecting Dickinson's exposure to the new phenomenon of wartime photography, "My Portion is Defeat – today –" has deservedly become a touchstone[20] for demonstrating the power and originality of Dickinson's Civil War writing:

> My Portion is Defeat – today –
> A paler luck than Victory –
> Less Paeans – fewer Bells –
> The Drums dont follow Me – with tunes –
> Defeat – a somewhat slower – means –
> More Arduous than Balls –
>
> 'Tis populous with Bone and stain –

And Men too straight to stoop again –
And Piles of solid Moan –
And Chips of blank – in Boyish Eyes –
And scraps of Prayer –
And Death's surprise,
Stamped visible – in stone –

There's somewhat prouder, Over there –
The Trumpets tell it to the Air –
How different Victory
To Him who has it – and the One
Who to have had it, would have been
Contenteder – to die –   (*Fr 704A, in Fascicle 33*)

As Ed Folsom observes, the technological limitations of 1860s photography "led to a photographic record of the Civil War that emphasized preparations for and aftereffects of battles, instead of the actual battles themselves. There are no photographs of Civil War battles, but there are many photos of soldiers and officers before battles, of dead corpses on the fields, and of wounded soldiers in hospitals."[21] In its focus on the aftermath of battle Dickinson's poem strictly honors these limitations of the new medium, making no attempt to visualize in figurative language the battle that the photography of her time could not let noncombatants see. Instead, as Eliza Richards put it, Dickinson "contrasts the capacities of poetic and photographic expression by rendering visible states of mind that photography may be able to register but cannot explicate."[22] Dickinson sees in the photographic record what can no longer be heard: "Piles of solid Moan," individual death coagulating into mass death in the battle's aftermath. And she identifies an invisible and unheard aftermath of battle, the secret shame of the "One" survivor and the homefront noncombatant, both in their different ways separated from the collective music of victory as well as from the photograph's witness to mass death.

According to Richards, Dickinson's Civil War poems "repeatedly posit an insurmountable gap between civilians' vicarious experience of the war, gained through newspaper reports and pictorial representations, and soldiers' direct, physical and largely unimaginable experience of combat."[23] "My Portion is Defeat – today –" and "It feels a shame to be Alive –" do so explicitly; in other poems, the very uncertainty of Dickinson's reference to the war points to that same insurmountable gap. When Dickinson projects "Whole Gulfs – of Red, and Fleets – of Red – / And Crews – of solid Blood –" into a spectacular sunset (Fr 468, around 1862), it seems entirely plausible that her mind's eye was recalling and transforming popular "pictorial representations" of the war such as Frederic Church's painting *Our Banner in the Sky* (1861), which projects a battle-torn American flag into a dramatic sunset landscape of red cloud bands and blue star-field.[24] If so, Dickinson's re-mediation of Church's painting both points to the bloodshed sublimated by Church and acknowledges its own doubly distanced relationship to the conflict. A distant "Drama – / That bows – and disappears –," Dickinson's bloody sunset shocks but remains beyond any spectator's ability to touch or influence.

And yet the American Civil War was in its time and place a total war, the only one ever fought within the continental territory of the United States, more deadly for those enlisted in the fighting and more costly in terms of absolute numbers of deaths than any fought by the United States before or since. Eliza Richards reads "The name – of it – is 'Autumn'" as Dickinson's attempt to write this total war in a way that documentary photography never could: "Dickinson's poem ... warns readers that the slaughter on the battlefront sprinkles, soaks, and floods the people at home; blood is not only on their hands, it is in their bonnets and in their streets."[25] Between the war's overwhelming force and Dickinson's keen awareness of her distance from it, however, her readers may never be certain of where to draw the boundaries of Dickinson's Civil War poems. Recalling that balloons were deployed for battlefield surveillance during the Civil War, Renée Bergland speculates that "You've seen Balloons set – Haven't You" too, is a kind of war poem, concerned with the problem "of witnessing imperial spectacles of violence from afar."[26] Hearing an echo of Lincoln's prophecy for the "house divided" in Dickinson's "The Props assist the House," we might wonder whether Dickinson's poem expresses some hope on behalf of the United States that the house the Framers built might yet prove adequate to its conception. If not – if the perfected Life's refusal of social belonging seems too absolute to serve as an image for hope at the level of the nation – does that poem's image of perfect self-sufficiency take on added weight as a refusal of the kinds of collective belonging and feeling summoned by modern war?

Refusal of collective demands was something Dickinson excelled at, even in wartime: early in the Civil War she refused to roll bandages, weave blankets, or make boots, and she persistently declined appeals from her friend Samuel Bowles to contribute her writing to fundraising efforts on behalf of wounded veterans.[27] Nevertheless, her stance in many of the poems of 1861–1865 seems closer to that of Marianne Moore and H. D. in World War II, who could neither disavow the war's aims nor forget their noncombatant status, than to the contempt of much World War I poetry for what Wilfred Owen famously called "The old Lie: Dulce et Decorum est / Pro patria mori." Like Marianne Moore's "In Distrust of Merits" (1942), Dickinson's "My Portion is Defeat" asks of the poet not whether she believes in the war, but rather, in Moore's words, "am I / what I can't believe in?"[28] Between Dickinson's photographic Civil War and her readers today lie not only World War I's disillusionment but also World War II's newsreels, a war in Vietnam beamed nightly into American television sets, and more recently, as Bergland observes, drone-based war experienced as a video game in real time, blowing up enemy targets at a distance even while graphic images of the dead, like those Dickinson saw in Civil War photographs, become ever more rare.[29] Rather than bringing us closer to the Civil War, the distinctive value of Dickinson's wartime poetry lies in her willingness to turn her critical eye on her own privilege of distance.

Set down in 1861, somewhere near the beginning of the Civil War, "The Robin's my Criterion for Tune –" envisions a less horrific, less coercive, less dissolving kind of national belonging than do Dickinson's most explicit war poems. Nationhood as Dickinson imagines it in this poem hews closely to Benedict Anderson's famous account of modern liberal nations as "imagined communities": collectivities understood to be "both inherently limited and sovereign," defined by territorial boundaries within which citizenship is ideally "conceived in language, not blood."[30] Seeing "New Englandly," Dickinson prizes the limitations that produce the world's plural linguistic, aesthetic, and political sovereignties. She represents these generative limitations as acquired, not innate; were she born in England rather than in Massachusetts she would have seen different landscapes differently and acquired different figural languages. She represents them at the same time as relative, not absolute limitations: one can be "taught" the elements of another nation's language, literature, and culture. As Anderson observes, it always remains possible in principle, within the boundaries of human finitude and capacity to acquire languages, to join the chorus of another nation[31] – to exchange the tune of the Robin for that of the Cuckoo, or vice versa, in Dickinson's terms. Falling short of full acquisition of another nation's language and experience, it remains possible to translate between them, Dickinson affirms – to understand the ways in which "Robin" and "Cuckoo" occupy equivalent places in different national landscapes and national poetries. "The Robin's my Criterion for Tune –" asserts that aesthetic value is both locally rooted and identified in comparative perspective.

In the world we now inhabit, it seems inevitable that we prize the connections between Dickinson's New England and the wider world, as well as the value brought to Dickinson's writings posthumously by her international readership. Nothing would seem more provincial now than to read Dickinson's poetry only for the supposed purity or special intensity of its American inheritance. As Masako Takeda observes in a recent anthology on *The International Reception of Emily Dickinson*, the Emily Dickinson Society of Japan was established in 1980, several years earlier than the Emily Dickinson International Society's founding in the United States.[32] Christopher Benfey has also charted the interchanges between New England and Japan during Dickinson's lifetime and during the posthumous emergence of her writing. Noting that "[t]he successive spikes in her reputation – during the 1890s, the 1920s, and the 1950s – correspond to periods of heightened American awareness of Asian culture," he argues that "[f]or a hundred years and more, American readers have read and interpreted Dickinson's work through a Japanese lens."[33] When the Emily Dickinson International Society held its 2007 international conference in Kyoto, scholars compared Dickinson's stylistic compression to that of traditional Japanese verse forms such as haiku; compared the history of elite Japanese women's "pillow books" and coterie writing to Dickinson's pattern of circulating her poetry in familiar correspondence; and explored American modernism's simultaneous embrace of Japanese culture and Dickinson's work.[34] In all these ways Japan has helped interpret Dickinson to American and other English-speaking readers.

Dickinson has also helped interpret Japanese society to itself. In the aftermath of the 2011 Tohoku earthquake and tsunami, a Japanese newspaper printed a short poem by Dickinson as both emblem and explanation of widespread Japanese reluctance to parade suffering before the world's gaze. "After several sleepless nights of worries and fears of aftershock I opened the newspaper," recalls Tokyo-based Dickinson scholar Naoki Onishi, "and found a Japanese translation of a poem by Emily Dickinson quoted in a popular column entitled 'Vox Populi Vox Dei,' of the *Asahi Simbun*, the major national newspaper" – in its original English, this quatrain:

> Unto a broken heart
> No other one may go
> Without the high prerogative
> Itself hath suffered too
> > (*Fr 1745A*)

Cutting across popular and elite culture in three different languages – Latin, English, and Japanese – the *Asahi Simbun*'s translation of Dickinson's lines about the abiding "gap between a suffering person and one trying to console" allowed her Japanese readers to voice with diplomatic courtesy, in the words of the other, their own sense of their nation in this crisis as both broken and high.[35] Dickinson's circulation in Japan is only one translation of many that are now widening her value for a world readership and changing how she is read in her native land.

5 Faith and doubt

Anyone who knows any Dickinson poems probably knows "Because I could not stop for Death –." "If the word great means anything in poetry, this poem is one of the greatest in the English language," wrote the American poet and critic Allen Tate, one of Dickinson's most important early critical champions, in 1936; his judgment has since been ratified not only by innumerable anthology editors, but also by the several composers who have set the poem to music, from Aaron Copeland to Natalie Merchant.[1]

The poem Tate knew as "one of the greatest in the English language" was not, however, exactly the poem as Dickinson wrote it. A single manuscript copy of the poem survives, transcribed into one of Dickinson's fascicles around 1862. The only version available to Tate in 1936 was that published by Higginson and Todd as "The Chariot" in their first edition of Dickinson's poems. Compare it to Franklin's version, a century later:

THE CHARIOT

Because I could not stop for Death,
He kindly stopped for me;
The carriage held but just ourselves
And Immortality.

We slowly drove, he knew no haste,
And I had put away
My labor, and my leisure too,
For his civility.

We passed the school where children played,
Their lessons scarcely done;
We passed the fields of gazing grain,
We passed the setting sun.

We paused before a house that seemed
A swelling of the ground;
The roof was scarcely visible,
The cornice but a mound.

Since then 'tis centuries; but each
Feels shorter than the day
I first surmised the horses' heads
Were toward eternity.   (*Poems 1890*)

Because I could not stop for Death –
He kindly stopped for me –
The Carriage held but just Ourselves –
And Immortality.

We slowly drove – He knew no haste
And I had put away
My labor and my leisure too,
For His Civility –

We passed the School, where Children strove
At Recess – in the Ring –
We passed the Fields of Gazing Grain –
We passed the Setting Sun –

Or rather – He passed Us –
The Dews drew quivering and Chill –
For only Gossamer, my Gown –
My Tippet – only Tulle –

We paused before a House that seemed
A Swelling of the Ground –
The Roof was scarcely visible –
The Cornice – in the Ground –

Since then – 'this Centuries – and yet
Feels shorter than the Day
I first surmised the Horses' Heads
Were toward Eternity – (Fr 479A)

Higginson and Todd's editorial meddling here was significant. In the third stanza, they replaced Dickinson's off-rhyme of "Ring'"/"Sun" with the perfect, and perfectly clichéd, rhyme of "done" / "sun," added a near-rhyme in "played" / "grain," and bleached Dickinson's schoolchildren of their licensed, even compulsory, aggression. They omitted the poem's "Chill" fourth stanza altogether, and so passed over Dickinson's suggestion of the mortal body cooling and stiffening in death as well as the culmination of the poem's remarkable play with relative motion, which comes in the speaker's realization that it is she who is stilled while the warm sun and the living world move on from her. In the following stanza Higginson and Todd edited out the sunkenness of Dickinson's grave "in the ground," thus removing, as Helen Vendler points out, "the suggestion of the gradual subsidence of the body's 'House'" attending the decay of its physical contents – the "fact of physical dissolution" that Tate discerned even through Higginson and Todd's efforts to carve Dickinson's words into a consolatory shape. Dickinson's own version of the poem, in Vendler's summary, "is about the apprehension of real death, offering no rescue. ... Once possessed by this knowledge, Dickinson cannot (in this poem) return to a belief in personal Immortality."[2]

No immortality, only eternal death; no heaven and no God – in this great poem, and in its many variants throughout the body of Dickinson's writing. "I heard a Fly buzz – when I died –" (Fr 591, circa 1863) begins another famous poem from a posthumous speaker, in which the impending decay of the body and the shutting down of its senses ("And then the Windows failed – and then / I could not see to see –") displace the orthodox revelation looked for by both the dying person and those keeping vigil. The moment "when the King / Be witnessed – in the Room –" never arrives; no escort of angels attends the dying person to heaven; only the fly's "Blue – uncertain – stumbling Buzz" remains to usher the speaker out of consciousness. A companion poem to "I heard a Fly buzz –" records from the perspective of those keeping watch over the body's death what happens when the King fails to "Be witnessed – in the Room –":

> 'Twas warm – at first – like Us –
> Until there crept opon
> A Chill – like frost opon a Glass –
> Till all the scene – be gone.   (Fr 614A, ll. 1–4, circa 1863)

Still another famous poem begins in the perspective of the dead, laid to rest in their sunken houses. As Vendler observes, this poem "emphasizes the buried body"[3] over the hope of a resurrection that may never come:

> Safe in their Alabaster Chambers,
> Untouched by morning –
> And untouched by noon –
> Lie the meek members of the Resurrection –
> Rafter of satin – and Roof of stone –
>
> Grand go the years – in the Crescent – above them –
> Worlds scoop their Arcs –
> And Firmaments – row –
> Diadems – drop – and Doges – surrender –
> Soundless as dots – on a Disc of snow –   (Fr 124C, circa 1861)

The coffined dead are safe from the fly's blue buzz but not from bodily dissolution, and the grave's claustrophobic "Roof of stone" is what the dead cannot lift if they would – "I wanted to get out," says the dead boy speaking in another poem, "'Twas just this time, last year, I died" (Fr 344, circa 1862), "But something held my will." Dickinson's dead boy still thinks in human time and still hopes to be reunited with family and friends in heaven; "Safe in their Alabaster Chambers" extinguishes that conventional hope in an utterly different scale of time, indifferent to individual human connection and desire. In another poem, the grief-stricken mourner who tries to think of the coffin as a vessel of individual immortality sheltering "A Citizen of Paradise" finds instead that the grave's "restricted Breadth" is capable of swallowing the entire living world, leaving behind only "Circumference without Relief – / Or Estimate – or End –" (Fr 890, circa 1864).

What is the value of this grim vision? From one perspective, the answer seems obvious: this suite of poems about death replaces an illusion – belief in personal immortality and the resurrection of the body – with the truth of the body's dissolution and the endlessness of the grave. In this perspective, to value "Safe in their Alabaster Chambers" is to adopt Dickinson's graveyard resistance to all of the consolations of belief – in Helen Vendler's words, to take up Dickinson's stance as "the unbeliever commenting on the deluded faithful."[4] And yet most of the time Dickinson did not so crisply distinguish belief from unbelief and truth from delusion. If there is no God, only death, in these poems, Dickinson elsewhere in her poetry conjugates almost every other possible posture of belief and doubt. Some poems make God available in order to challenge his justice. Many poems posit a God jealous of the earthly happiness of his creatures, especially their human loves; from time to time this God relents. Like any devil citing scripture, Dickinson likes to use God's own words against him:

> If "God is Love" as he admits
> We think that he must be
> Because he is a "jealous God"
> He tells us certainly
>
> If "All is possible with" him
> As he besides concedes
> He will refund us finally
> Our confiscated Gods –   (Fr 1314C, ll. 33–40)

When offering consolation to others, Dickinson sometimes did extend a hope of immortality or envision God as a benevolent if remote power. Toward the end of her life she sent the following short poem to several recipients, often in acknowledgment of mutual bereavements, as when she enclosed it in a letter to Judge Otis Lord's executor, Benjamin Kimball, at some point following Lord's death in March 1884:

> Though the great Waters sleep
> That they are still the Deep,
> We cannot doubt.
> No vacillating God
> Ignited this Abode
> To put it out. *(Fr 1641F)*

It appears from one of her several letters to Kimball (perhaps, but not certainly, the one enclosing this poem) that Dickinson had inquired about the circumstances of Lord's death and received from Kimball an account indicating that Lord had met his end without struggle, but without the hope or expectation that "the King / Be witnessed – in the Room –."[5] "Perhaps to solidify his faith was for him impossible," Dickinson mused in reply, "and if for him, how more, for us! ... Neither fearing Extinction, nor prizing Redemption, he believed alone. Victory was his Rendezvous – I hope it took him home" (*Letters* 968). Neither fearing extinction nor prizing redemption, Dickinson's short poem returns to the beginning of all things, God's ignition of heaven and earth in Genesis (KJV 1:1–2). From out of the darkness upon the face of the deep she brings forward a ground note of belief in the endurance of God and God's creation, and nothing more. During Dickinson's own final illness in 1886, she incorporated the same poem into another letter to a grieving friend, with the reflection that "Though the first moment of loss is eternity other eternities remain" (*Letters* 1036).

Dickinson is treasured by many readers as a religious poet, and perhaps by just as many as a poet of radical skepticism in matters of faith. Although both are partial, neither sense of ownership is simply wrong, even if what James McIntosh calls Dickinson's "nimble believing" – "believing for intense moments in a spiritual life without permanently subscribing to any received system of belief" – I would be more inclined to call her nimble doubt, her "theologically answerable doubt" as Elisa New puts it.[6] Although she stood apart while her Mount Holyoke classmates and members of her own family affirmed their faith and were received into the church, Dickinson never fixed herself permanently in the posture of the lonely skeptic superior to the "deluded" believers. Her many and memorable blasphemies almost always take the part of human solidarity with the things of this earth against divine absence or vindictiveness, returning time and again to their starting point in "The Fact that Earth is Heaven – / Whether Heaven is Heaven or not" (Fr 1435, circa 1877). Starting from the premise that Earth is Heaven, Dickinson could envision Immortality as a gift extended not by God but by one human being to another: "To 'know in whom' we 'have believed', is Immortality," Dickinson wrote to friends in 1884 (Fr 1669). The Pentateuch may be no more than a "Romance," as Dickinson calls the Bible in another poem, Moses only a fictional character whose historical reality "in soberer moments" she doubts, but Dickinson's sympathetic identification with Moses's human plight brings him to life for her as a injured victim of God's will to demonstrate his own power: "Old Man on Nebo! Late as this – / My justice bleeds – for Thee!" (Fr 521, circa 1863).

Dickinson shared with many of her intimate correspondents poems and letters written out of her abiding disposition to judge divine things by human standards. The following famous poem went to her nephew Ned, perhaps at a time when he was kept home at the Evergreens by illness, with the introductory line "'Sanctuary Privileges' for Ned, as he is unable to attend –." :

The Bible is an antique Volume –
Written by faded Men
At the suggestion of Holy Spectres –
Subjects – Bethlehem –
Eden – the ancient Homestead –
Satan – the Brigadier –

> Judas – the Great Defaulter –
> David – the Troubadour –
> Sin – a distinguished Precipice
> Others must resist –
> Boys that "believe" are very lonesome –
> Other Boys are "lost" –
> Had but the Tale a warbling Teller –
> All the Boys would come –
> Orpheus' Sermon captivated –
> It did not condemn –   (Fr 1577C, around 1882)

Considered simply as a "Tale" written by men, a book among others catalogued on a dusty shelf, the Bible, Dickinson suggests, is reasonably full of incident but lacks charm. As Ned would have recognized, his aunt's *precis* of the Bible's narrative high points maps them onto Amherst village life, centered on the Dickinson family Homestead and radiating outward to encompass the stock characters of any small New England town: the overbearing Brigadier (a word Dickinson attached to the "shrill" and "civic" neighborhood blue jay in another late poem, Fr 1596B, that she sent next door to Susan Dickinson); the ne'er-do-well bankrupt, the local poet (Dickinson's own role in Amherst's social economy). The Bible borrows its plotlines, Dickinson suggests, from the things of this earth; where Jonathan Edwards saw the natural world as the image or shadow of divine things, Dickinson sees Eden as the "faded" image or shadow of Amherst. Her ambiguous note's reference to "sanctuary privileges" (was Ned unable to attend church services, or to visit Dickinson herself?) invites Ned to find refuge or asylum in Dickinson's generous unbelief rather than in orthodox Christianity.

The sermon of unbelief does better to captivate than condemn. In McIntosh's words, Dickinson's poetry of "nimble believing" characteristically finds an "appropriate form" and an "assured tone, maintained amid its shifting thought."[7] In a poem such as "The Bible is an antique Volume –," the tonal challenge Dickinson faces is that of juxtaposing experienced human time against received sacred time without reductionism – without allowing unbelief to make its objects small or her style mean, as she feared it could:

> Those – dying then,
> Knew where they went –
> They went to God's Right Hand –
> That Hand is amputated now
> And God cannot be found –
>
> The abdication of Belief
> Makes the Behavior small –
> Better an ignis fatuus
> Than no illume at all –   (Fr 1581A, circa 1882)

"The Bible is an antique Volume –" meets this challenge by encompassing the Bible within the experiential space of literacy itself. The opening lines of the poem invoke the homely infinitude of the library; the inventory of the Bible's "Subjects" gestures toward the world of the romance or the novel, oriented to character and plot. (To read a meaty nineteenth-century novel is usually to watch someone or other fall off Sin's distinguished precipice; as Vendler observes, this poem's "humorously colloquial" cast of characters "reminds us that Dickinson and Mark Twain were contemporaries."[8]) The poem's closing lines remind readers of the legend of the Pied Piper of Hamelin, who drew the children of the village after him while their parents were occupied in church, and invoke the "warbling" generic bird of lyric song, before calling on Orpheus, whose song captivated all created things, to bless this teller and her tale. Behind all of these specific and generic allusions Dickinson would have expected her readers to recall the words of Jesus in the Gospels, "Suffer the little children to come unto me, and forbid them not, for of such is the kingdom of God" (March 10:14, KJV). Come unto me and be "lost" is Dickinson's counter-invitation: lost as a Boy might be in a book or in the library, where readers of poetry – in Samuel Tayler Coleridge's famous definition – "transfer from our inward nature a human interest and a semblance of truth sufficient to procure for these shadows of imagination that willing suspension of disbelief for the moment, which constitutes poetic faith."[9]

In Dickinson's eyes, the received forms of religious belief also had their own power to make their objects small. Her writings are typically scornful of prayer – "We pray – to Heaven – / We prate – of Heaven –" (Fr 476, circa 1862) – and especially so of what theologians call "petitionary prayer," the direct appeal to God for some boon or mercy. As set forth by Jonathan Edwards in "The Most High a Prayer-Hearing God" (1736), petitionary prayer posits a God who is "infinitely above all and stands in no need of creatures, yet he is graciously pleased to take a merciful notice of poor worms of the dust." Although prayer serves above all "as an offering to him," and although prayer's chief rewards chiefly lie in glimpsing God's "glorious grace, purity, sufficiency, and sovereignty" rather than in any direct grant of a petitioner's request, from time to time this remote God "manifests his acceptance" of his creature's prayers "by *doing* for them agreeable to their needs and supplications[,] ... by causing an agreeableness between his providence and their prayers."[10]

Dickinson seems to have experienced every last atom of this theology as a provocation. Where Edwards extols petitionary prayer as both an offering to and an experience of God's immense majesty, Dickinson represents it as an instrumental transaction diminishing to both parties:

> Prayer is the little implement
> Through which Men reach
> Where Presence – is denied them –
> They fling their Speech
> By means of it – in God's Ear –
> If then He hear –
> This sums the Apparatus
> Comprised in Prayer –   (Fr 623A, circa 1863)

As Jed Deppmann observes, this little poem "activates, in compressed lyrical form, an unresolved dialectic between the two unattractive entities of a sardonic, secular, scientific consciousness and a flailing, hapless Christianity."[11] In Dickinson's poem it is God himself who seems infirm, in need of a sort of cosmic ear trumpet – diminished rather than glorified by his distance from his creatures. Toward the end of her life Dickinson drafted a letter to Helen Hunt Jackson, her friend and fellow poet, expressing her concern for Jackson's slow recovery from a broken leg along with her own inability to petition God on Jackson's behalf:

> Knew I how to pray, to intercede for your Foot were intuitive –
>   but I am but a Pagan.
> Of God we ask one favor, that we may be forgiven –
> For what, he is presumed to know –
> The Crime, from us, is hidden –
> Immured the whole of Life Within a magic Prison
> We reprimand the Happiness
> That too competes with Heaven –   (Fr 1675B, circa March 1885)

Dickinson's God, in this poem, is needier than his creatures. Content with the happiness bounded by mortal life, human beings have nothing to ask of God except forgiveness on the trumped-up charge of preferring earth to heaven; like a parent's reprimand to a restless child on a visit of social duty, the object of prayer is to protect God from the knowledge that we would really rather be somewhere else. As one criminal to another, Dickinson sent to her nephew Ned the following direct parody of prayer:

> "Heavenly Father" – take to thee
> The supreme iniquity
> Fashioned by thy candid Hand
> In a moment contraband –
> Though to trust us – seem to us
> More respectful – "We are Dust" –
> We apologize to thee
> For thine own Duplicity –   (Fr 1500A, circa 1879)

For Jonathan Edwards, "grace, purity, sufficiency, and sovereignty" belong to God alone; in Dickinson's parody, the graciousness is all on the side of we poor worms of the dust.

These poems were not Dickinson's private blasphemies. Many of them were shared in correspondence. Dickinson's unprofessed faith was a matter of public fact in Amherst, evident whenever she stayed away from church or left before the communion service, and she lost no time in sharing her unbelief with Thomas Wentworth Higginson, to whom she sent "Some keep the Sabbath going to Church – / I keep it, staying at Home –" (Fr 236C, July 1862) early in their correspondence.[12] The value of these poems – their affirmation of human solidarity under protest – is also, however their limitation: if prayer is a "little implement," at some point parody and protest, as reactive forms, cannot exceed the size of their object.

Occasionally Dickinson explored the capacity of prayer to answer more transcendent purposes. The following poem – copied into a fascicle around 1863 but never, as far as we know, shared with any correspondent – meets Edwards' theology of prayer at least halfway:

> My period had come for Prayer –
> No other Art – would do –
> My Tactics missed a rudiment –
> Creator – Was it you?
>
> God grows above – so those who pray –
> Horizons – must ascend –
> And so I stepped upon the North
> To see this Curious Friend –
>
> His House was not – no sign had He –
> By Chimney – nor by Door –
> Could I infer his Residence –
> Vast Prairies of Air
>
> Unbroken by a Settler –
> Were all that I could see –

Infinitude – Had'st Thou no Face
That I might look on Thee?

The Silence condescended –
Creation stopped – for me –
But awed beyond my errand –
I worshipped – did not "pray" –   (*Fr 525A, circa 1863*)

The poem begins in the transactional or instrumental space of little prayer, with the speaker picking up one tactic and another in an effort to negotiate some unspecified crisis, only to find that all but prayer have failed her. Instructed that "God grows above" – her imperfect, literal-minded recollection of a lesson heard about an immortal being – she climbs to look North, a direction that Dickinson associated both with secular poetic vocation, "invoke[d]" by the North in "God made a little Gentian –" (Fr 520), and with religious martyrdom, whose "Needle" points steadfast "thro' polar Air" (Fr 187). Lifting her eyes to the hills (Dickinson would have expected her readers to recognize the template of Psalm 121 informing this poem[13]), she opens up her initially narrow perspective by great leaps of negation, moving from the scale of the village street (where she seeks and cannot find God's house or door) to the "Unbroken" continent to "Infinitude." There, like Moses asking God to show him his glory (Exodus 33:18–23 KJV), she asks to see Infinitude's face, and, like Moses, she has her petition granted in part. Where Moses sees the "back parts" but not the face of God's glory, "for there shall no man see me, and live," Dickinson experiences a revelation that may or may not come through the searching eye of the poem's first four stanzas. "The Silence condescended" – she does not say it spoke; "Creation stopped" – she does not say that something filled the pause. What she can testify to is the enlarged character of her own response: "I worshipped – did not 'pray' –."

In Dickinson's poem as in Jonathan Edwards' sermon, the central reward of prayer is the witnessing of self-sufficient, sovereign infinitude rather than the granting of any particular boon. Dickinson's poem, however, artfully detaches this final revelation from the hope of seeing a personal God like the one she prayed to "first, a little Girl, / Because they told me to –" (Fr 546), an anthro-pomorphic God who

> . . . looked around,
> Each time my Childish eye
> Fixed full, and steady, on his own
> In Childish honesty –
>
> And told him what I'd like, today,
> And parts of his far plan
> That baffled me –
> The mingled side
> Of his Divinity –   (Fr 546A, ll. 5–13, circa 1863)

Edwards' "Prayer-Hearing God" does not show his face to Dickinson, still less his back parts, when she lifts her eyes unto the hills. This poem rejects prayer for the sake of worship, which Dickinson defines as the experience of awe before an "Infinitude" immanent in Creation itself. What "Because I could not stop for Death" takes away, this poem restores: Creation stops for her, and yet she lives.

By contrast with her energetic repudiation of prayer, Dickinson found in the vocabulary of the Christian sacraments more promising forms of belief and unbelief. Where prayer in the Protestant tradition of Dickinson's upbringing accentuated God's infinite distance from his "poor worms of the dust," the two Protestant sacraments – baptism and the Eucharist – made God's grace visible through earthly signs and memorialized the sojourn of Jesus Christ on earth – his sacrificial decision to love humanity in human form, knowing his love could never fully be returned:

> "They have not chosen me" – he said –
> "But I have chosen them"!
> Brave – Broken hearted statement –
> Uttered in Bethleem!

I could not have told it,
But since Jesus *dared,*
Sovereign, know a Daisy
Thy dishonor shared!

(*Fr 87B, circa 1859*)

The verse Dickinson quotes in this poem (John 15:16, KJV) directly follows Christ's command to his apostles at the Last Supper to "love one another, as I have loved you" and his declaration that the apostles are not servants, "for the servant knoweth not what his lord doeth: but I have called you friends; for all things that I have heard of my Father I have made known unto you" (John 15: 12, 15). Dickinson's Christ bears the shame of unrequited love in order to close the distance between God and his creatures and ratifies her own high valuation of human love, whatever its earthly outcome.

Dickinson adapted the imagery of the Lord's Supper – "Christianity's quintessential act of memory" as W. Clark Gilpin calls it[14] – to sacralize her earthly commitments. In Helen Vendler's summary, she "appropriated the Incarnation as a metaphor for her own experience of the 'consent of Language'" (in Fr 1715, "A Word made Flesh is seldom / And tremblingly partook") and accordingly analogized the act of reading to the communion service ("He ate and drank the precious Words – / His Spirit grew robust –," Fr 1593; "Strong Draughts of Their Refreshing Minds / To drink – enables Mine," Fr 770).[15] The words of a treasured but infrequent correspondent arrive "like signal esoteric sips / Of the communion Wine" (Fr 1476). The lovers united and separated in "There came a Day at Summer's full" (Fr 325) are "Permitted to commune this – time – / Lest we too awkward show / At supper of the Lamb." The speaker of "These are the days when Birds come back –" knows what follows upon the "blue and gold mistake" of Indian summer, but willingly suspends her disbelief long enough to petition for admission to summer's "Last Communion in the Haze" (Fr 122).

However qualified, these are all poems of affirmation. Indian summer's seeming permanence is a "Fraud," but its beauty is not; a jealous God in the background may constrict the lovers' earthly connection, but cannot undermine the value Dickinson assigns to it;

Dickinson's sacralization of human love and natural time competes with orthodox religious faith but is not wholly incompatible with it. In other poems, though, Dickinson connects the imagery of the Lord's Supper to hungers utterly forbidden or unappeasable, altogether outside of sacramental resolution. As Vendler observes, "The theme of the unsubduable appetite for flesh prompts some of Dickinson's best imaginative efforts":

> As the Tiger eased
>
> By but a Crumb of Blood, fasts Scarlet
> Till he meet a Man
> Dainty adorned with Veins and Tissues
> And partakes – his Tongue
>
> Cooled by the Morsel for a moment
> Grows a fiercer thing
> Till he esteem his Dates and Cocoa
> A Nutrition mean
>
> I, of a finer Famine
> Deem my Supper dry
> For but a Berry of Domingo
> And a Torrid Eye –   (Fr 1064A, circa 1865)

Noting that Dickinson applied "Domingo" and "Torrid" to Susan Gilbert Dickinson (in a letter sent to Susan around 1883, *Letters* 855), Vendler sees this poem as "suggest[ing] how thoroughly the acquaintance with Susan spoiled her for milder fare."[16] This poem's desacralizing hunger wants only what it wants, accepting no substitutes and allowing for no transfiguration. It would turn the Word back into Flesh if a poem could do so – if Dickinson's "dry" conclusion did not keep it leashed within the bounds of a "Berry of Domingo," on a diet of mere symbolic sips of the communion wine.

Worse than unappeasable hunger, though, is none at all. The same sacramental vocabulary that Dickinson cannibalizes to render her voracious Tiger she uses elsewhere to figure the utter collapse of desire:

> I had been hungry, all the Years –
> My Noon had Come – to dine –
> I trembling drew the Table near –
> And touched the Curious Wine –
>
> 'Twas this on Tables I had seen –
> When turning, hungry, Home
> I looked in Windows, for the Wealth
> I could not hope – for Mine –
>
> I did not know the ample Bread -
> 'Twas so unlike the Crumb
> The Birds and I, had often shared
> In Nature's – Dining room –
>
> The Plenty hurt me – 'twas so new –
> Myself felt ill – and odd –
> As Berry – of a Mountain Bush –
> Transplanted – to the Road –
>
> Nor was I hungry – so I found
> That Hunger – was a way
> Of persons Outside Windows
> The entering – takes away –   (Fr 439A, circa 1862)

According to Vendler, "This emotionally naked poem," figured as a "secular Communion" of bread and wine, "allegorizes any and all sorts of mistaken desire: for fame, for marriage, for any dreamed-of satisfaction."[17] Naked it is, but I'm less certain that this poem is centrally concerned with mistaken desire, a problem that might be cured by a different choice of object. The negative space that Dickinson carves out in this poem becomes clearer when set against a more orthodox devotional poem that Dickinson may well have known, George Herbert's "Love (III)" from his collection *The Temple* (1633):

> Love bade me welcome: yet my soul drew back,
>   Guiltie of dust and sinne.
> But quick-ey'd Love, observing me grow slack,
>   From my first entrance in,
> Drew nearer to me, sweetly questioning,
>   If I lack'd any thing.
>
> A guest, I answer'd, worthy to be here:
>   Love said, you shall be he.
> I the unkind, ungratefull? Ah my deare,
>   I cannot look on thee.
> Love took my hand, and smiling did reply,
>   Who made the eyes but I?
>
> Truth Lord, but I have marr'd them: let my shame
>   Go where it doth deserve.
> And know you not, says Love, who bore the blame?
>   My deare, then I will serve.
> You must sit down, sayes Love, and taste my meat:
>   So I did sit and eat.[18]

Herbert's "Love" throws into stark relief the most fundamental deprivation in Dickinson's secular communion: her poem's dinner lacks a host. Herbert's poem takes the form of a dialogue between Christ and the poem's sinful, self-conscious narrator, in which Christ's gracious love will not be denied; Dickinson's poem explores the internal division of a self that recalls but can no longer experience its previous hungers, and there appears to be no interlocutor in the poem with whom she can share this diminishment. Her narrator's shame is not one of self-maiming sin, as it is for Herbert's diffident guest; her former subsistence as a companion of the birds and guest of Nature to all appearances was innocent (Dickinson is no more persuaded of original sin in this poem than in "Of God we ask one favor"). If guilt belongs to those whose windows so long shut her out, they remain invisible and inaccessible. The "ample" objects of desire sit in front of her, but desire's conditions of possibility are absent in a world where no reciprocating eye (no "Torrid Eye" like that recalled in Fr 1064) returns her gaze.

So far as we know, Dickinson never shared "I had been hungry, all the Years –" with any correspondent in her lifetime: fittingly, since in this poem both sacred and secular communion fail her. This poem admits doubt into the very sanctuary of Dickinson's secular faith: her assertion of human solidarity in loving and memorializing the things of this earth. And yet her doubts dignify rather than diminish her. The doubting, experienced narrator of "I had been hungry, all the Years –" occupies a larger space and deploys an ampler style, in the poem's initial and closing stanzas, than does her earlier self. In the present culture of public religion in the United States, where the space afforded to doubt is pressed upon from many sides, Dickinson's willingness to doubt her own secular faith as well as the more orthodox religious traditions around her still captivates and enlarges.

6   The Spirit lasts – but in what mode –

Put it this way, as a thought experiment: If somehow all of Dickinson's manuscripts were lost along with all the copies of all the print editions and all the facsimiles, analogue and digital, of her writings – if Dickinson's poetry had to be reconstructed like Sappho's, from the memories of readers, from a smattering of fragments quoted by other writers, and from the assembled shards of Emily Dickinson coffee mugs occasionally unearthed from office middens – I suspect that an astonishing share of the corpus of her work could be accurately reassembled in stanza form, on its most basic metrical scaffolding of sound and sense.

Other aspects of Dickinson's writing that readers now value, however, including its embeddedness in personal correspondence and the visual appearance of her manuscripts, would be much harder to reconstruct. The affinity between particular poems and the wording of memorable letters; the poems that Dickinson chose to include in her first outreach to Thomas Wentworth Higginson; the high points of her long correspondence with Susan Gilbert Dickinson – readers would likely be able to converge on these. Reconstructing what was already a twentieth-century editorial reconstruction, experts might be able to reach a tolerable degree of consensus on the original relationship of the poems in at least some portions of some fascicles. In the effort to assemble and compare reliable texts of the poems, readers would contribute to recollecting Dickinson's most striking variant readings; it would be interesting to see how many such readings could be attested to by multiple readers. Readers who had spent time with Dickinson's manuscripts or their reproductions would retain, I think, at least general visual templates of early, middle, and late Dickinson: the careful cursive of the earliest fascicles, the wider spacing, cross-marked variants and unpredictable line breaks of the mid-1860s, the exploded fragments of the later years – and in the absence of the original manuscripts, memory would inevitably be biased toward the most extreme and distinctive characteristics of each phase of the life of Dickinson's writing. Memory of particular visual line breaks in particular poems in most cases would decay far more quickly. The most striking forms of individual letters in Dickinson's handwriting might linger in the mind's eye and be recreated by artists, but again as general visual templates, I suspect, rather than as meaningful components of specific poems; trying to remember the particular slant of a dash or elongation of an "s" in relation to any given poem's words would exhaust human capacities.

The point of my thought experiment is this: the Dickinson left to us by this imaginary calamity, although grievously diminished, would still matter to us, and what is central to her literary value would, I think, be preserved. Dickinson's poetry engrafts itself deeply into her readers by means of humankind's most ancient aural technologies of memory: rhythm, rhyme, assonance, and repetition. The convergence and clash of rhyme, rhythm, sound, and lexical sense are more fundamental to Dickinson's art than the sometimes felicitous tension produced by the visual line breaks running athwart metrical patterns in her manuscript poems. It's true that when Dickinson wrote to Susan Gilbert Dickinson,

> Show me Eternity, and I will show you Memory –
> Both in one package lain
> And lifted back again –   (Fr 1658A, Letters 830)

she identified "Memory" with the material conditions of her manuscript writing, laid away in keepsake boxes by her beloved correspondents. Between one re-reading of her letter-poem and the next, however, what would have preserved these lines in Susan's memory and what makes them memorable now is the near-rhyme of "Eternity" with "Memory," reinforcing the syntactical parallelism of the first line; the rhyme of "lain" and "again"; and the internal rhyme of "package" with "back again." These mnemonic patterns of sense and sound are the ones that both Johnson and Franklin recognized in setting aside most of the manuscript's visual line breaks to print these words as a three-line stanza, and it seems to me that they grasped what was most valuable about Dickinson's writing in doing so.[1] In the bifurcation of present-day Dickinson studies between readers who make the case for Dickinson as a proto-modernist poet oriented to the visual line on the page and those who hear her metrical forms sounding in intimate dissonance with those of her surrounding culture, I believe the weight of evidence falls with those who, like Cristanne Miller, argue that Dickinson "writes a poetry of implied orality," one "more crucially attuned to the ear than to the eye," at the very least through the mid-1860s and likely beyond. Dickinson along with her contemporaries, as Miller asserts, "regarded the poem as an essentially aural structure, which could be performed or mapped in distinct and various ways in writing."[2]

I want to be careful here, though. Dickinson's poetry of "implied orality" flourished in a world of what Walter J. Ong famously describes as secondary rather than primary orality, "a more deliberate and self-conscious orality, based permanently on the use of writing and print."[3] Her world was saturated with both manuscript writing and print (the Dickinson household subscribed to some fifteen periodicals in the 1860s).[4] Her own compositional process, as Alexandra Socarides most recently has explored in depth, was shaped by the material conditions of writing that she found at hand in her culture and that she in her turn deliberately shaped, both in handcrafting her fascicles and in her selection, later in life, of the writing surfaces that Holland Cotter describes as "stained with life."[5] Looking at the late jottings inside an envelope that R. W. Franklin pieces together as a quatrain "followed by five lines that are at least related in part," it's impossible to think that composition for Dickinson was just a process of transcribing an aural form already fully formed in her head:

> When what they sung for is undone
> Who cares about a Blue Bird's Tune –

Why, Resurrection had to wait
Till they had *moved a stone   * Could move a Stone

As if *a Drum went on and on   *the Drums
To captivate the slain –

I dare not write until I hear –
Intro without my Trans –

When what they sung for is undone   (Fr 1545A)[6]

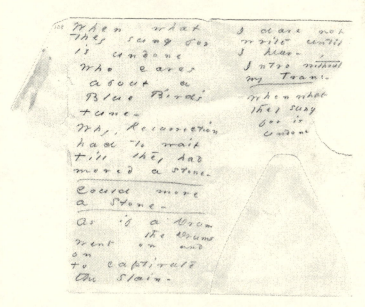

By permission of Amherst College Archives and Special Collections

Seeing her words on the page, aligning them with her paper's folds, delineating alternative stabs at her topic, returning to her opening words and copying them again rather than simply reading them off from their initial inscription: whatever aural form Dickinson held in mind while setting down these lines, it was clearly mediated by the process of putting intelligible marks on the page, "based ... on the use of writing," in Ong's words. Yet even in this visually striking manuscript Dickinson honors the ancient convention likening poetry to song; she asserts the primacy of aural pattern in composition – "I dare not write until I hear" – and rigorously observes one of the most commonplace aural patterns in English verse, iambic meter. Phrase boundaries provide syntactical cues, reinforced by the off-rhymes of "undone," "Tune," and "stone," for grouping those iambs into metrically regular lines of four and three feet. Anyone literate in English can resurrect Dickinson's Tune from its written marks (as Franklin did in editing this manuscript for print), and having done so, may remember it more vividly in its aural form.

Or so my thought experiment argues. And as it happens, evidence for my thought experiment may be found elsewhere in the remaining contemporary records of Dickinson's writing. One of the several surviving witnesses of "Safe in their Alabaster Chambers" is a partial transcript of the poem's first stanza, made by an unknown hand, passed down in Mabel Loomis Todd's papers and now preserved at Amherst College. It's possible that the transcript is faithful to a lost manuscript version of the poem shared by Dickinson herself with a correspondent now unknown, but more likely, as R. W. Franklin believes, that this text's divergence from all the other known versions of the poems indicates that it was "recalled, unreliably, from memory" by the transcriber:

> Deep in their alabaster chambers,
> Untouched by morn and untouched by noon,
> Sleep the mute members of the Resurrection
> Roof of satin and rafter of stone,   (Fr 124G)[7]

Much of Dickinson's poem survives in this recollected version, and something is lost. This writer's substitution of "Deep" for "Safe" (in all other, better-attested surviving versions of the poem) preserves the meter and something of the sense of the first line, but forfeits the alliteration on "s" sounds that helps bind the stanza together. The writer's substitution of "mute" for "meek" preserves the alliteration, and much of the sense, of Dickinson's "meek members" (in all other surviving versions). The transcript scrambles, however, the pairs of words that Dickinson tightly linked through assonance – *Rafter* of *satin* and *Roof* of *stone*. It disrupts as well the meter of this final line, which in Dickinson's own versions of this stanza contrasts the first half of the line, two metrical feet beginning with strong stresses (a dactyl followed by a trochee) – a comparatively rapid, forward-moving aural pattern – with the two emphatic iambs that conclude both the line and the stanza as a whole on strong stresses, falling with the weight of stone. Along with the other variant readings in this transcript, this metrical fumbling suggests a poetically inexpert ear, but hardly an ear of stone; rather, one that was assisted in its imperfect work of memory by Dickinson's poetic architecture of sound and sense. Both the errors of this transcription and what it manages to retain demonstrate the enduring power – mnemonic and aesthetic – of the multiple, mutually reinforcing aural patterns that Dickinson exploited in her poetry.

Dickinson seems to reflect on her aural architecture, and on its enabling conditions of secondary orality, in a gnomic poem transcribed into Fascicle 35 around 1863. The distinction drawn in this poem between the "smaller ear" and "the Conscious Ear" echoes that drawn in "The Brain – is wider than the Sky –" (Fr 598) between "Syllable" and "Sound":

> The Spirit is the Conscious Ear –
> We actually Hear
> When we inspect – that's audible –
> That is admitted – Here –
>
> For other Services – as Sound –
> There hangs a smaller Ear
> Outside the Castle – that Contain –
> The other – only – Hear   (Fr 718A)

We do not hear, Dickinson writes, until we "inspect" – etymologically, "look in." "Actually" hearing a poem entails more than registering its sounds faithfully; discriminating between "Here" and "Hear" requires inspection, a mental architecture of signification, not just a functioning sensory apparatus. Dickinson suggests that this kind of "Conscious" hearing may be actively assisted by written inscription (whether in manuscript or in print), which can distinguish graphically between syllables registered identically by the "smaller Ear." The "Conscious Ear" is where poetry sounds, even if only in the "implied orality" (in Cristanne Miller's terms) of silent reading, drawn from the written or printed page.

Ong speculates that the invention of print, which made written works ever "smaller and more portable" and more affordable, "set[] the stage psychologically for solo reading in a quiet corner, and eventually for completely silent reading" – a "major factor," according to Ong, "in the development of the sense of privacy that marks modern society."[8] Nineteenth-century American observers of these developments, like the great Unitarian preacher William Ellery Channing, both asserted and hoped that "the diffusion of these silent teachers, books" would generalize the conditions of individual "self-culture": "Instead of forming their judgments in crowds, and receiving their chief excitement from the voice of neighbors, men are now learning to study and reflect alone."[9] Dickinson's poem concisely sums up this great turn in the history of literacy and individual identity. In the famous dictum of English common law, a man's house is his castle; for Emily Dickinson, a lawyer's daughter, the silent reader's brain is her castle.

On the face of it, "The Spirit is the Conscious Ear" endorses a kind of philosophical idealism, elevating the "Conscious" spirit over the merely serviceable senses and, by extension, the abstract lexical significance of a poem over its sensory medium or media, whether those media address themselves to the ear or to the eye. Dickinson's privileging of "Spirit" over the sensory things of this earth, however, was rarely so unequivocal; earth would always be heaven for her, whether heaven was heaven or not. The Castle's little ear of a knocker or doorbell, hanging outside for such "Services – as Sound –," is a faintly ridiculous and faintly pathetic image, suggesting the claims of the denigrated body and the sensory poetic medium (in this instance

once again Dickinson's favored "common meter," the popular hymn
or ballad stanza alternating four-stress and three-stress iambic lines,
rhymed *abcb*) through which it humbly speaks. Who or what might
wait outside the haughty castle of the sovereign self-cultured individual, petitioning for admittance? In a later poem, it is a "Vital Word"
from life itself that restores the spirit and the body to one another, as
equals, through the medium of the senses:

> I heard, as if I had no Ear
> Until a Vital Word
> Came all the way from Life to me
> And then I knew I heard –
>
> I saw, as if my Eye were on
> Another, till a Thing
> And now I know 'twas Light, because
> It fitted them, came in.
>
> I dwelt, as if Myself were out,
> My Body but within
> Until a Might detected me
> And set my Kernel in –
>
> And Spirit turned unto the Dust
> "Old Friend, thou knowest Me",
> And Time went out to tell the News
> And met Eternity   (*Fr 996A, circa 1865*)

This poem's topic is recovery, from depression as we would say today:
from depression's anhedonia and rumination, the absent but obsessive
introspection that sees nothing it looks upon. Echoing and contrasting
with the posthumous speaker of "I heard a Fly buzz – when I died"
(Fr 591), who at the point of life's extinction "could not see – to see,"
this poem narrates a resurrection of body and spirit into the life of this
world. The poem repeats this core narrative a biblical three times,
beginning with the recovery of the senses of hearing and sight and

concluding with the restoration of "Myself," the "Kernel" of identity. (The Spirit's address to the body in this poem, "thou knowest me," alludes to and reverses Peter's thrice-repeated denial – "I do not know the man" – of Jesus Christ after his arrest; see Matthew 26:69–74, KJV). Breath or flame would be more orthodox metaphors than "Kernel" for the spirit dwelling in the body; Dickinson's choice of this concrete, palpable, discrete emblem for the core of her being, like the narrative arc of the poem as a whole, underlines the "Vital" dependence of spirit on the life of the sensate, bounded, individual body. The poem's aural pattern and its visual inscription together memorialize this joint resurrection of "Spirit" and "Dust," especially so in the remarkable enjambments of the second stanza, where the line breaks suggest the vacancy of the mind unmoored from its worldly objects and groping for words until met by a "Light" that seems "fitted," exactly measured, to its bodily eyes.[10] Dickinson's poetic stanza, a closely "fitted" and nevertheless more flexible container than the "Castle" of "The Spirit is the Conscious Ear," holds together the time before and the time after, absence and recovery, death and resurrection.

Dickinson almost always distrusted assurances of immortality apart from the body – certainly when it came to beloved human beings, but also, I suspect, in thinking of poetry and its media. Writing a note of consolation to a distant relative on the loss of his daughter, Dickinson envisioned a Heaven "not so unlike Earth that we shall miss the peculiar form – the Mold of the Bird –" (*Letters* 671; Fr 1537). Personal immortality may often have seemed illusory to Dickinson, but it was the only kind of immortality that ever mattered to her. Along with other of her scientifically informed contemporaries, Dickinson both hoped for a resurrection of the specific, "peculiar," fiercely individual body and wondered how such a resurrection could be possible, after ashes returned to ashes and dust to dust. She read in her school books and was reminded in works such as Edward Hitchcock's *Religious Lectures on Peculiar Phenomena in the Four Seasons* (delivered as lectures during Hitchcock's distinguished tenure as President of Amherst College and published in 1850) that human bodies "suffer entire decomposition, and that the ultimate elements are scattered by the wind and the waves, and are taken up by other bodies." In response to this problem, Hitchcock proposed that "some infinitesmal germ" surviving of the earthly body might suffice to "constitute the germ of the spiritual body," as a small seed can reconstitute the entire plant.[11] Hitchcock's "germ of the spiritual" may have made its way into Dickinson's image of the resurrecting "Kernel" of continuous human biographical identity; both "germ" and "Kernel" partake of matter and spirit without being reducible to either one. Like the "Mold of the Bird" that Dickinson hopes to recognize in heaven, Hitchcock's "germ" and Dickinson's "Kernel" have the power to resurrect the "peculiar form" of an material body without literally reconstituting that body atom for atom.

From the perspective of our own day, what empowers Hitchcock's "germ" as well as Dickinson's "Kernel" and "Mold" is that each is a bearer of what we now call *information*: the genetic information stored in the seed and expressed in the plant, the information stored in the mold's template and reproduced in casting from it (the definitions of "mold" in Dickinson's dictionary include both "the matter of which anything is formed" and "the matrix in which anything is cast and receives its form"[12]). What the resurrection of the body has in common with the survival and transmission of a poem is that each is fundamentally a problem of communication – that is, "of reproducing at one point either exactly or approximately a message selected at another point," as the mathematician Claude Shannon famously defined "communication" in a paper sometimes credited with launching the Information Age.[13] To pose the problem in Dickinson's own words: The spirit lasts – but in what mode?

> The Spirit lasts – but in what mode –
> Below, the Body speaks,
> But as the Spirit furnishes –
> Apart, it never talks –
> The Music in the Violin
> Does not emerge alone
> But Arm in Arm with Touch, yet Touch
> Alone – is not a Tune –

The Spirit lurks within the Flesh
Like Tides within the Sea
That makes the Water live, estranged
What would the Either be?
Does that know – now –
Or does it cease –
That which to this is done,
Resuming at a mutual date
With every other one?
Instinct pursues the Adamant,
Exacting this Reply,
Adversity if it may be, or wild Prosperity,
The Rumor's Gate was shut so tight
Before my Mind was sown,
Not even a Prognostic's Push
Could make a Dent thereon –   (Fr 1627B)

Dickinson sent these lines in October 1883 to Charles H. Clark, with whom she corresponded following the death of the Reverend Charles Wadsworth (Clark's brother James had been Wadsworth's lifelong friend and wrote to Dickinson upon Wadsworth's death; Dickinson was "speechlessly grateful for a friend who also was my friend's" and picked up the correspondence with Charles Clark when James too died in February 1883; see *Letters* 804). In addition to Wadsworth, Dickinson and her family in October 1883 were mourning her nephew Gilbert Dickinson, Susan and Austin Dickinson's son, who died that month, at eight years of age, of typhoid fever. If ever Dickinson wanted to believe wholeheartedly in personal immortality, or to comfort others with its assurance, it must have been in October 1883. Although she wrote Susan in the days immediately following the disaster that "Expanse cannot be lost," she acknowledged finding "The Rumor's Gate" of heaven shut tight to her; those whom Gilbert left behind were "Moving on in the Dark like Loaded Boats at Night," where "though there is no Course, there is Boundlessness" (*Letters* 871).

Returning to "The Rumor's Gate" in "The Spirit lasts – but in what mode –," Dickinson was no more able than before to write with conviction of heaven or the resurrection.[14] The poem's tortured middle lines, with their surfeit of impersonal pronouns (*that, it, one*), figure the "mutual date" of the Resurrection as a "Resuming" that befalls an immense and lonely crowd (as Dickinson previously pictured it in "No Crowd that has occurred," Fr 653), rather than as a joyful family reunion. What Dickinson does return to with some conviction in this poem is poetry. Like the violin's tune, like the ocean's tides – like every other signifying pattern that we have learned to call "information" – poetry depends utterly on its material medium without being reducible to it. Dickinson here cannot imagine – indeed, apparently does not wish to imagine – any human spirit or aesthetic form "estranged" from its medium. What would the Tides be, estranged from the Sea? And "yet Touch / Alone – is not a Tune –"; the pattern that constitutes any given "Tune" might be translated into another medium – touched at the piano rather than by the violin, or even digitally synthesized – while retaining its essential form. The same, Dickinson implies, may be true of both persons and poems. As a tune is not reducible to "Touch / Alone," a poem is not reducible to its material artifact. With respect to persons, this poem remains open to the possibility that the "peculiar forms" of individual identity, Dickinson's beloved "Mold of the Bird," could likewise be communicated into media other than the ones we know on earth. In the signifying excess of "Tune" over "Touch" lies all that Dickinson can credit of immortality on this side of the adamant.

The spirit lasts, but in what mode? The thought experiment I posed at the beginning of this chapter – imagine reconstructing Dickinson's poetry from the collective memory of her readers, unassisted by any mnemonic technologies other than rhythm and rhyme – runs counter to much scholarly work on Dickinson today, which is increasingly dedicated to importing her manuscript writings, with ever greater sophistication and completeness, into our very latest visual technologies of memory. The public interest in Dickinson's manuscripts that Mabel Loomis Todd first stimulated, when she reproduced "There came a Day – at Summer's full –" in facsimile in the 1891 *Poems, Second Series*, continues to grow in parallel with, and assisted by, the efforts of scholars and editors. Beginning with Martha Nell Smith's launch of the Dickinson Electronic Archives at the University of Maryland in 1994, the ever-expanding availability of bandwidth for transmitting images, and ever-improving digital techniques and conventions for tagging and searching them, further stimulated readerly demand for viewing Dickinson's writings online and in the seeming immediacy of high-fidelity digital reproduction rather than in print editions. So compelling had this demand become by the first decade of this century that Harvard University and Amherst College, the two major repositories of Dickinson's surviving manuscripts after family tensions – the notorious "War between the Houses" fueled by Austin Dickinson's long affair with Todd – splintered her literary remains, managed to set their differences aside long enough to collaborate in assembling the Emily Dickinson Archive. Meanwhile, the scholars on the project's editorial board, myself among them, managed to set our differences aside long enough to produce a minimal scholarly apparatus for orienting readers new to Dickinson's manuscripts.[15]

Compiled through Harvard University's Houghton Library and opened to public viewing in October 2013, the Emily Dickinson Archive offered readers for the first time a unified portal, equipped with powerful search tools, through which to access digital images, thoroughly indexed and accompanied by Franklin's editorial transcriptions, of almost all of Dickinson's surviving manuscript poems. Sooner rather than later, its architects hope, Dickinson's surviving letters in their entirety (not just the poems embedded in her letters, or those strings of words in her letters that an editor has decided are poems) will become part of the electronic archive as well, thus enabling readers around the world to choose for themselves how much or how little credence they will place in Franklin's sense of where a letter ends and poem begins, or in his assembly of a cockeyed, cancellation-ridden late fragment into a coherent stanza. Readers today can reasonably look forward to seeing Dickinson's manuscript writings in their entirety as never before.

The Emily Dickinson Archive entered the world on the heels of another revelation in Dickinson studies, the announcement in August 2012 of a possible new daguerreotype of Emily Dickinson. To date, the daguerreotype has met every authenticating test put to it over several years by the Jones Library of Amherst College, which received a copy from the daguerreotype's then owner in 2007 and was presented with the original in 2013, and by Martha Nell Smith, who has also been researching the image.[16] The daguerreotype appears to show a Dickinson nearer to thirty years of age than twenty, seated alongside and with her arm behind the chair of another woman who has been identified as Katherine Scott Anthon Turner, the recipient of some intimate letters from Dickinson from their 1859 meeting in Amherst, during a visit Turner made to Susan Dickinson, through 1866, when Turner remarried. The daguerreotype may vindicate the scholarship of Rebecca Patterson, who in *The Riddle of Emily Dickinson* (1951) identified Kate Turner as Dickinson's beloved during the crucial years of the early 1860s. If it is authenticated, this image also will let readers see the adult Dickinson, at the peak of her productivity, as they never have before.

Compared to the hooplah surrounding previous purported Dickinson likenesses, though – the albumen photograph released by Philip Gura in 2000 and the photograph included in Richard Sewall's *Life of Emily Dickinson* (1974), both generally now viewed as discredited[17] – the reception of this latest image seems muted. One reason may still be widespread, unspoken reluctance to acknowledge Dickinson's erotic yearnings toward women. The more powerful reason is surely simple caution, given the track record of previous claims to have found a new image of Dickinson. Even when not adulterated with frills, curls, and mascara, the surviving daguerreotype of the sixteen-year-old Dickinson is so unsatisfying – "solitary, staring out, and a bit fretful," in the characterization of the Dickinson Electronic Archives, the image of a young woman seemingly uncomfortable in her own skin – that the itch to replace it has occasionally overwhelmed the skepticism of the most rigorous historical scholars.

What serious reader of Dickinson would not be drawn to the possibility of replacing that too-familiar icon with the picture of "a bold, assertive woman in her twenties" (as she appears to the editors of the Dickinson Electronic Archives) or, with a slightly different emphasis, that of "a mature woman showing striking presence, strength and serenity," who seems to be in charge of the occasion (as she is seen by the curators of the daguerreotype at Amherst College)?[18] If the identification and dating of the daguerreotype hold up, it was made near the time of Dickinson's concerted self-dedication to her poetic vocation. That the strong woman in this image is gesturing possessively toward another woman imbues the daguerreotype's implicit narrative with that much more power and that much more danger, as the scholars examining it are well aware. Viewers see in the image the Dickinson we want most urgently to see, and the daguerreotype could not be better constructed to appeal to readers' desires to see and possess a biographical Dickinson more equal to the boldness of her writing, and nearer in time to the flood years of her work. With all due caution, Amherst College continues to invite viewers who may know anything of the daguerreotype's background to come forward, whether their evidence "is favorable or unfavorable to the proposed identification of the image as Emily Dickinson and Kate Scott Turner"; and so this new image remains in something of a scholarly limbo, from which it may or may not emerge vindicated.

I wonder whether the daguerreotype, as it awaits further judgment, is losing ground against the ever-more-available images of Dickinson's manuscript hand in competition for our attention. More speculatively, I also wonder whether the hyperbolic value currently placed on *all* of these digitally mediated Dickinsonian images is sustainable in its present form. The foundational digital projects of the 1990s in Dickinson studies made it their aim, in representing her manuscripts online, to "prioritize the physical object over the logical lexical content."[19] As I have argued in this chapter and elsewhere, I do not believe that prioritizing writing's physical object over its lexical content fully reflects Dickinson's own aesthetic aims, practices, and theory of her poetry in relationship to its aural and graphic media – a question that concerned Dickinson deeply, as manuscript scholars have helped us appreciate and value. To quote Holland Cotter once more: "conveyed in whatever medium, words are the fundamental matter of her art, what it is about, and what Dickinson was about."[20] Usage statistics for the Emily Dickinson Archive in its first year of operation seem to bear this out: the most frequently visited pages on the site are not those presenting Dickinson's most visually arresting writings, but rather those of great and familiar poems, including "Because I could not stop for Death" and "My Life had stood – a Loaded Gun –," whose manuscripts are comparatively tame.[21] Looking to the near future of Dickinson studies, I agree with Cristanne Miller that the aural Dickinson is overdue for a return, and along with the aural Dickinson, the lexical and philosophical Dickinson represented in the recent work of scholars such as Jed Deppman and Michelle Kohler.[22] In this book, I have tried to demonstrate the value of a reading experience in which Dickinson's words are what startle most.

Something of value, though, remains in our lingering gaze upon Dickinson's manuscript writings and the other visual traces of her life. Given the unpublished condition of her poetry during her own lifetime, Dickinson's manuscript materials are and will remain of compelling interest to readers, and the challenge of editing them will be renewed for succeeding generations in ways that no one now alive can predict. As more and more nineteenth-century manuscript archives come online – the New York Public Library launched its Shelley-Godwin archive, presenting digital reproductions of the manuscripts of Mary Wollstonecraft, William Godwin, Percy Shelley, and Mary Wollstonecraft Shelley, within days of the Emily Dickinson Archive launch[23] – the circumstances surrounding Dickinson's writing and its posthumous life will lose, usefully, something of their exceptionalist aura in being joined to wider awareness and appreciation for how nineteenth-century manuscript practices interfaced with print culture. Virginia Jackson is surely right that no reader of Dickinson's surviving manuscripts can ever hope "to return to a moment before Dickinson's work became literature, to discover within the everyday remnants of a literate life the destiny of print."[24] Still, I expect that readers will continue to be drawn to those remnants, both for their witness to Dickinson's uniquely talented literate life and as objects to think with about the fast-changing conditions of everyday literate life in the present.

What is the destiny of print? Call this question one of historical rather than literary value if you like, but that division seems to me unhelpful for valuing Dickinson's poetry in the long perspective. My newest Kindle™ no longer shows me Dickinson's face, retouched or otherwise: the screensaver's rotation of authorial portraits has been replaced with pictures of writing technologies – ranks of pencils, fountain pens, typewriter keys, and vintage wooden typefaces. Something is changing in the nature of authorship and in our embodied relationship to writing, and this change contributes to our heightened awareness of the conditions in which Dickinson copied and circulated her manuscript poetry. To visit the Emily Dickinson Archive or any other electronic archive of digital surrogates for Dickinson's manuscripts is to feel the widening distance between Dickinson's writing life, during which manuscript entwined itself around print and the typewriter was born, and our own emerging culture of the digital image, if it is not already too late to call it "emerging." (Mabel Loomis Todd in 1887 taught herself to type on a borrowed typewriter, copied of few of Dickinson's manuscript poems for Lavinia Dickinson to demonstrate this intriguing new technology, and in doing so persuaded Lavinia that she, rather than Susan Dickinson, was more likely to help skeptical editors discover the destiny of print latent within Dickinson's "peculiar handwriting."[25]) Just as ancient Greek literary culture was energized for centuries by debate over the impact of writing on poetry's mnemonic technologies of rhythm and rhyme, it is both exhilarating and sobering now to grasp poetry's long passage through aural forms, manuscript, print, and digital reproduction through the prism of Dickinson's magnificent oeuvre.

Notes

INTRODUCTION

1. Emily Dickinson Historic Vinyl Wall Graphic Decal Sticker, www .amazon.com/WGH58082-Dickinson-Historic-Graphic-Historical/ dp/B008LoNKUS/ref=pd_sim_sbs_misc_6, accessed June 25, 2013.
2. Mabel Loomis Todd, "Preface," in Thomas Wentworth Higginson and Mabel Loomis Todd, eds., *Poems by Emily Dickinson*, Second Series (Boston: Roberts Brothers, 1891), 5–6.
3. Susan Howe, *The Birth-Mark: Unsettling the Wilderness in American Literary History* (Hanover: University Press of New England, 1993), 134.
4. Sharon Cameron, *Choosing Not Choosing: Dickinson's Fascicles* (Chicago: University of Chicago Press, 1992).
5. M. L. Rosenthal and Sally M. Gall, *The Modern Poetic Sequence: The Genius of Modern Poetry* (New York: Oxford University Press, 1983); and for a subtle reading of Fascicle 16 as a response to the Civil War, Paula Bernat Bennett, " 'Looking at Death, is Dying': Fascicle 16 in a Civil War Context," in Paul Crumbley and Eleanor Elson Heginbotham, eds., *Dickinson's Fascicles: A Spectrum of Possibilities* (Columbus: Ohio State University Press, 2014), 106–29.
6. Marta Werner, *Radical Scatters: Emily Dickinson's Late Fragments and Related Texts, 1870–1886*, http://jetson.unl.edu:8080/cocoon/ radicalscatters/default-login.html, accessed July 9, 2013, n.p.
7. Robert Weisbuch, *Emily Dickinson's Poetry* (Chicago: University of Chicago Press, 1975), 19.
8. Virginia Jackson, *Dickinson's Misery: A Theory of Lyric Reading* (Princeton: Princeton University Press, 2005), 52, 51.
9. Martha Nell Smith, *Rowing in Eden: Rereading Emily Dickinson* (Austin: University of Texas Press, 1992), 1–2.
10. R. W. Franklin, "Introduction," *The Poems of Emily Dickinson: Variorum Edition*, Vol. 1 (Cambridge, MA: The Belknap Press of Harvard University Press, 1998), 27.

11. www.hup.harvard.edu/features/dickinson/ (Cambridge, MA: Harvard University Press), accessed July 5, 2013. Emily Dickinson Archive, www.edickinson.org/.

12. Jackson, *Dickinson's Misery*, 53.

13. See Jed Deppman's *Trying to Think with Emily Dickinson* (Amherst: University of Massachusetts Press, 2008), for an arresting illustration of the brain as dissected in a mid-nineteenth-century anatomy text-book (97) and on Dickinson's awareness more generally of moral philosophy's concern for the relationship between mind and brain (75–108).

I THE LIFE OF DICKINSON'S WRITING

1. Lawrence Lipking, *The Life of the Poet: Beginning and Ending Poetic Careers* (Chicago: University of Chicago Press, 1981), 11, 10.

2. Edward Said, *On Late Style: Music and Literature Against the Grain* (New York: Pantheon Books, 2006), 3.

3. Helen Vendler, *Coming of Age as a Poet: Milton, Keats, Eliot, Plath* (Cambridge, MA: Harvard University Press, 2003), 1.

4. Lipking, *Life of the Poet*, 10.

5. Said, *Late Style*, 6, 148.

6. David Porter, *Dickinson: The Modern Idiom* (Cambridge, MA: Harvard University Press, 1981), 5.

7. Albert Habegger, *My Wars Are Laid Away in Books: The Life of Emily Dickinson* (New York: Random House, 2001), xiii, xiv.

8. Todd, "Preface," *Poems* Second Series, 6.

9. Habegger, *My Wars Are Laid Away in Books*, xiii.

10. Cristanne Miller, *Reading in Time: Emily Dickinson in the Nineteenth Century* (Amherst: University of Massachusetts Press, 2012), 6.

11. On Dickinson's eye treatments of 1864–1865 in relation to the fascicles, see Franklin, *Poems*, 25; on the Dickinson household servants and Dickinson's productivity in these years, see Aïfe Murray, *Maid as Muse: How Servants Changed Emily Dickinson's Life and Language* (Hanover, NH: University Press of New England, 2010), 78–81.

12. Franklin, *Poems*, 27.

13. Erik Gray, *The Poetry of Indifference: From the Romantics to the Rubaiyat* (Amherst: University of Massachusetts Press, 2005), 2.

14. Habegger, *My Wars Are Laid Away in Books*, 526.

15. Jen Bervin and Marta Werner, eds., *The Gorgeous Nothings: Emily Dickinson's Envelope-Poems* (New York: Christine Burgin/New Directions, 2013).

16. Marta Werner, "Fly Leaves," in *Ravished Slates: Revisioning the "Lord" Letters*. Available at www.emilydickinson.org/ravished-slates-re-visioning-the-lord-letters, n.p., accessed February 1, 2015.

17. Holland Cotter, "A Poet Who Pushed (and Recycled) the Envelope" (rev. of Jen Bervin and Marta Werner, eds., *The Gorgeous Nothings*), "Books of the Times," *New York Times*, December 6, 2013, C32.

18. For a brief on behalf of the aesthetic interest of the envelope manuscript of "The Mushroom is the Elf of Plants," see Sally Bushell, "Meaning in Dickinson's Manuscripts: Intending the Unintentional," *Emily Dickinson Journal* 14.1 (2005): 47–52; and for a counterargument that the shape of Dickinson's envelope poems "facilitates the physical act of writing by allowing Dickinson a confined space in which to write without material interruption" but is otherwise not meaningful, see Domhnall Mitchell, *Measures of Possibility: Emily Dickinson's Manuscripts* (Amherst and Boston: University of Massachusetts Press, 2005), 197–200.

19. On "The Circus Animals' Desertion" as "a falling from [Yeats's] ladder of sublimation," see Helen Vendler, *Poets Thinking: Pope, Whitman, Dickinson, Yeats* (Cambridge, MA: Harvard University Press, 2004), 117.

20. Franklin, *Poems*, 11.

21. I will occasionally be placing more trust in Franklin's reconstruction of the order of the sheets comprising each fascicle than would some readers. There can be no debate, of course, about the order and association of poems copied onto a single fascicle sheet. I am persuaded by Franklin's argument that "[u]sually the available evidence is substantial and mutually corroborative" concerning the internal sequence of any given fascicle's poems. R. W. Franklin, *The Manuscript Books of Emily Dickinson* (Cambridge, MA: The Belknap Press of Harvard University Press, 1981), xiv.

22. Cameron, *Choosing Not Choosing*, 105.

23. Mabel Loomis Todd, ed., *Poems by Emily Dickinson: Third Series* (Roberts Brothers, 1896), 33.

24. Helen Vendler, *Dickinson: Selected Poems and Commentaries* (Cambridge, MA: Harvard University Press, 2010), 27.

25. Seamus Heaney, "Digging," *Death of a Naturalist* (1966; repr. London: Faber & Faber, 1988), 13.

26. On the manuscript sheet as Dickinson's unit of composition, see Alexandra Socarides, *Dickinson Unbound: Paper, Process, Poetics* (New York: Oxford University Press, 2012), 20–48.

27. Cameron, *Choosing Not Choosing*, 34.

2 SOME STRIDING – GIANT – LOVE –

1. "Yet, love, mere love, is beautiful indeed / And worthy of accepta-tion"; Sonnet X of "Sonnets from the Portuguese," marked with a wavy pencil line in the Dickinson family library copy of Elizabeth Barrett Browning's *Prometheus Bound, and Other Poems* (New York: C. S. Francis; Boston: J. H. Francis, 1851); EDR 525, Houghton Library of Harvard University, Cambridge, MA.

2. William Shurr, *The Marriage of Emily Dickinson: A Study of the Fascicles* (Lexington: University Press of Kentucky, 1983).

3. Paula Bennett, "The Pea that Duty Locks: Lesbian and Feminist-Heterosexual Readings of Emily Dickinson's Poetry," Karla Jay and Joanne Glasgow, eds., *Lesbian Texts and Contexts: Radical Revisions* (New York: New York University Press, 1990), 104–25.

4. James Merrill, *The Book of Ephraim*, in *Divine Comedies* (New York: Atheneum, 1980), 47.

5. Werner, *Ravished Slates*, Installation 4, n.p.

6. Werner, *Ravished Slates*, "Fly Leaves," n.p.

7. Werner, *Ravished Slates*, "Fly Leaves," n.p.

8. Vendler, *Poems and Commentaries*, 133.

9. Linda Freedman, *Emily Dickinson and the Religious Imagination* (Cambridge and New York: Cambridge University Press, 2011), 103.

10. Elizabeth Phillips, *Emily Dickinson: Personae and Performance* (University Park: Pennsylvania State University Press, 1988), 113.

11. Mabel Loomis Todd's editorial notebook places the poem in Fascicle 11. It survives only in a transcript made by Todd's assistant Harriet Graves, the original manuscript having been cut away from its surviv-ing companion leaf, bearing "What would I give to see his face?" (Fr 266).

12. Shurr, *Marriage of Emily Dickinson*, 15, 60, versus Elizabeth Maddock Dillon, *The Gender of Freedom: Fictions of Liberalism and the Literary Public Sphere* (Stanford: Stanford University Press, 2004), 242.

13. David Halperin and Valerie Traub, eds., *Gay Shame* (Chicago: University of Chicago Press, 2010), 3–48; Sandra Runzo, "Dickinson, Performance, and the Homoerotic Lyric," *American Literature* 68.2

(June 1996), 352–55; Michael Davidson, "Introduction: Women Writing Disability," *Legacy: A Journal of American Women Writers* 30.1 (January 2013), 2–3.

14. Eve Kosofsky Sedgwick, *Epistemology of the Closet* (Berkeley and Los Angeles: University of California Press, 1990), 67–90.

15. Laura Green, *Literary Identification from Charlotte Brontë to Tsitsi Dangarembga* (Columbus: The Ohio State University Press, 2012), 102.

16. The "Master" letters use both masculine and neuter pronouns, but never feminine pronouns, in characterizing their addressee; the first sentence of the third letter, for example, records Dickinson hesitating between "his" and "its" (*Letters* II: 391). Martha Nell Smith and others have nevertheless seen Susan Dickinson as a candidate for Dickinson's Master (Smith, *Rowing*, 130–53); alternatively, Smith speculates that the letters "may be all that remains of an extensive literary project devoted to fictional epistolary representation" (*Rowing* 125). Leading male contenders include the Reverend Charles Wadsworth (see Habegger, *My Wars Are Laid Away in Books*, 416–19); *Springfield Republican* editor and family friend Samuel Bowles (see Judith Farr, *The Passion of Emily Dickinson* [Cambridge, MA: Harvard University Press, 1998]), and Otis Lord. Farr, who also assesses carefully the importance of "The Narrative of Sue" (100–77) alongside Bowles in Dickinson's erotic life, usefully stresses that "the presence of one love does not cancel the power of the other," and suggests that Dickinson's figures of the beloved man and the desired woman "may usefully be compared so as to reveal the larger narrative of Dickinson's experience of love" (184).

17. "Although the sequence of events will no doubt always be obscure, it is thought Dickinson was taken to the Arch Street Presbyterian Church [during her stopover in Philadelphia in March 1855] to hear the Reverend Charles Wadsworth, and that he made such an impression on her she later solicited his counsel and thus initiated one of her most vital friendships. . . . It is also certain the poet corresponded with him before he moved to San Francisco in 1862." Habegger, *My Wars Are Laid Away in Books*, 330.

18. Habegger, *My Wars Are Laid Away in Books*, 520; Freedman, *Religious Imagination*, 103.

19. Vendler, *Poets Thinking*, 79, 76.

20. Ellen Louse Hart and Martha Nell Smith, eds., *Open Me Carefully: Emily Dickinson's Intimate Letters to Susan Huntington Dickinson*

(Ashfield: Paris Press, 1998) xxv, 256–57; see also Ellen Louise Hart, "The Encoding of Homoerotic Desire: Emily Dickinson's Letters and Poems to Susan Dickinson, 1850–1886," *Tulsa Studies in Women's Literature* 9.2 (Autumn 1990), 251–72.

3 WOMEN, NOW, QUEENS, NOW!

1. Lionel Trilling, *The Experience of Literature* (New York: Holt, Rinehart and Winston, 1967), 105–06.
2. This translation of Simonides' epitaph is by the British poet and cleric William Lisle Bowles (1762–1850); it circulated widely and Dickinson could have known the epitaph in this translation or in further translations derived from Bowles's.
3. Trilling, *The Experience of Literature*, 107.
4. Photographer Bill Swersey captured the banner for the *New York Times* the second time it was unfurled over Butler Library (September 25, 1989) as part of an authorized exhibition on women authors. The image subsequently headed many conference posters and furnished the cover of John Guillory's magisterial *Cultural Capital: The Problem of Literary Canon Formation* (Chicago: University of Chicago Press, 1993).
5. Trilling, *The Experience of Literature*, 106.
6. Todd, "Preface," *Poems*, Second Series, 5–6.
7. "The masquerade, in flaunting femininity, holds it at a distance": Mary Ann Doane, "Film and Masquerade," *Screen* 23.3-4 (September – October 1982), 81. Doane's essays on "Film and the Masquerade" and "Masquerade Reconsidered: Further Thoughts on the Female Spectator." *Discourse* 11.1 (Fall–Winter 1988–1989), 42–54, remain classic statements of this strand in 1980s feminist literary and cultural criticism. For further application to Dickinson's work, see Runzo, "Dickinson, Performance, and the Homoerotic Lyric."
8. Gregory Nagy, *The Ancient Greek Hero in 24 Hours* (Cambridge, MA: The Belknap Press of Harvard University Press, 2013), 410–14.
9. Tim Whitmarsh, *Narrative and Identity in the Ancient Greek Novel: Returning Romance* (Cambridge, MA: Cambridge University Press, 2011), 142.
10. Whitmarsh, *Returning Romance*, 143.
11. Yopie Prins, "'Lady's Greek' (With the Accents): A Metrical Translation of Euripides by A. Mary F. Robinson," *Victorian Literature and Culture* 34 (2006), 598.

12. The letter survived in fair copy among Dickinson's papers and is currently held at Amherst College. I have followed Thomas H. Johnson's editorial reconstruction in regarding as a single letter the several manuscript leaves cataloged as Amherst MS 742 and MS 744. A fair copy of a following note, also preserved at Amherst, suggests that Dickinson did send Lord at least something of her long letter of April 30–May 1: "I enclose the Note I was fast writing, when the fear that your Life had ceased, came, fresh, yet dim, like the horrid Monsters fled from in a Dream" (May 14, 1882, *Letters* 752).

13. Thomas Wentworth Higginson, "Ought Women to Learn the Alphabet?" *The Atlantic Monthly* 3, no. 16 (February 1859), 137–50.

14. Adrienne Rich, "Vesuvius at Home: The Power of Emily Dickinson" (1975; rpt. in *On Lies, Secrets and Silence: Selected Prose 1966–1978* [New York: W. W. Norton, 1979]), 172.

15. Susan Howe, *My Emily Dickinson* (Berkeley: North Atlantic Books, 1985), 110, 99, 35.

16. Rich, "Vesuvius at Home," 174.

17. Rich, "Vesuvius at Home," 174.

18. Rich, "Vesuvius at Home," 173, 174, emphasis mine.

19. Howe, *My Emily Dickinson*, 116.

20. Howe, *My Emily Dickinson*, 138. Notably, Rich's famous essay is acknowledged nowhere in *My Emily Dickinson*. Howe makes her extended argument with a female precursor who to all appearances "has been 'omitted, brushed aside at the scene of inheritances'" (*My Emily Dickinson*, 12) – to borrow Howe's own complaint about the French feminist theorist Hélène Cixous's neglect of Gertrude Stein.

21. Howe, *My Emily Dickinson*, 13.

22. As Virginia Jackson's reading of "My Life had stood –" emphasizes, *Dickinson's Misery*, 233–34.

23. Betsy Erkkila, *The Wicked Sisters: Women Poets, Literary History, and Discord* (New York and Oxford: Oxford University Press, 1992), 60.

24. Erkkila, *Wicked Sisters*, 62. Dickinson's relationship to the writing of her female contemporaries has been an important topic for readers ever since Higginson and Todd began to issue her work in print. For an early appreciation of Dickinson's interest in Emily Brontë, see Geneviève Taggard's *The Life and Mind of Emily Dickinson* (New York: A. A. Knopf, 1930). John Evangelist Walsh, in *The Hidden Life of Emily Dickinson* (New York: Simon and Schuster, 1971), fingered *Jane Eyre* and *Aurora Leigh* as the

catalytic works in Dickinson's literary emergence some years before Gilbert and Gubar's blockbuster *The Madwoman in the Attic* (1979). For retrospective analyses of 1970s–1980s feminist criticism connecting Dickinson to a tradition of women writers, see Erkkila, *Wicked Sisters* and Mary Loeffelholz, *Dickinson and the Boundaries of Feminist Theory* (Urbana and Chicago: University of Illinois Press, 1991).

25. Sylvia Plath, *Letters Home: Correspondence 1959–1963*, ed. Aurelia Schober Plath (London: Faber & Faber, 1975), 5, 110.

26. Sylvia Plath, *The Colossus and Other Poems* (1960, 1962; repr. New York: Vintage/Random House, 1998), 37–38.

27. Vendler, *Coming of Age as a Poet*, 126.

28. *The Unabridged Journals of Sylvia Plath*, ed. Karen V. Kukil (New York: Vintage Books, 2007), 93.

29. In an extended reading of Plath's relationship to other women writers, Stephen Axelrod argues that Plath's later and stronger poems "read Dickinson in such a way as to suggest that the precursor did not dare enough. In her most famous poems, Plath subverts the predecessor's rhetoric through programmatic intensification." *Sylvia Plath: The Wound and the Cure of Words* (Baltimore and London: The Johns Hopkins University Press, 1990), 128.

30. Sylvia Plath, "Ariel," in *Ariel* (New York: Harper & Row, 1965), 26.

31. Susan R. Van Dyne, *Revising Life: Sylvia Plath's Ariel Poems* (Chapel Hill and London: University of North Carolina Press, 1993), 126. Van Dyne's exploration of Plath's manuscript notebooks demonstrates that Plath revised "Ariel" to break up what were originally complete sentences in the poem's opening and to break down the draft's "initial dichotomy" between horse and rider (*Revising Life*, 121, 120).

32. The relationship between horse and rider in Plath's "Ariel" may have still more in common with that between the Owner and the gun in Dickinson's poem in light of Susan Stewart's recent speculation that "My Life had Stood –" may be a dramatic monologue spoken from the viewpoint of Dickinson's dog, Carlo. Although this reading in itself seems to me unhelpful, Dickinson, like Plath, may well have experienced her relationship with a beloved animal as an absorbing and rewarding way of thinking beyond human gender. Susan Stewart, "On ED's 754/764," *New Literary History* 45.2 (Spring 2014), 253–70. Stewart's essay also offers a useful summary of the massive interpretive history now surrounding "My Life had stood – a Loaded gun –."

4 HER AMERICAN MATERIALS

1. Ralph Waldo Emerson, "The Poet," in *Essays: Second Series* (Boston: James Munroe & Co., 1844), 40–41.
2. In Jane Austen's *Persuasion* (1818), Captain Wentworth takes "a beautiful glossy nut, which, blessed with original strength, has outlived all the storms of autumn" as his model for a woman who can hope to be "beautiful and happy in her November of life." *Persuasion* Vol. 1, chapter 10 (Cambridge and New York: Cambridge University Press, 2006), 94–95.
3. Vendler, *Poems and Commentaries*, 87.
4. Michelle Kohler, *Miles of Stare: Transcendentalism and the Problem of Literary Vision in Nineteenth-Century America* (Tuscaloosa: University of Alabama Press, 2014), 1–2.
5. Kohler, *Miles of Stare*, 2.
6. For a shrewdly comprehensive assessment of Dickinson's politics and those of her family, see Betsy Erkkila's "Dickinson and the Art of Politics," in Vivian Pollak, ed., *An Historical Guide to Emily Dickinson* (New York: Oxford University Press, 2004), 133–74.
7. Paul Crumbley, *Winds of Will: Emily Dickinson and the Sovereignty of Democratic Thought* (Tuscaloosa: University of Alabama Press, 2010), 17. Crumbley looks to find some redeeming space in Betsy Erkkila's portrait of Dickinson as "a witty and articulate spokesperson for an essentially conservative tradition, a late Federalist state of mind and sensibility" that fell out of the mainstream of American politics with the ascendancy of Thomas Jefferson and Andrew Jackson (Erkkila, "Art of Politics," 137).
8. Walt Whitman, *Leaves of Grass* (1855), in Michael Moon, ed., *Leaves of Grass and Other Writings by Walt Whitman* (New York: W. W. Norton, 2002), 671.
9. Vendler, *Poems and Commentaries*, 309.
10. Ralph Waldo Emerson, "Experience," in *Essays: Second Series*, 53.
11. Elizabeth Hewitt, *Correspondence and American Literature, 1770–1865* (Cambridge, MA: Cambridge University Press, 2004), 171.
12. Whitman, *Leaves of Grass* (1855), in Moon, ed., 692.
13. Suzanne Juhasz and Cristanne Miller, "Comic Power: A Performance," *The Emily Dickinson Journal* 5.2 (Fall 1996), 88.
14. Karen Haltunnen, *Confidence Men and Painted Women: A Study of Middle-Class Culture in America, 1830–1870* (New Haven: Yale University Press, 1982), 1–2, and Nancy Bentley, *Frantic Panoramas: American Literature and Mass Culture 1870–1920*

(Philadelphia: University of Pennsylvania Press, 2009), 1–5; William Dean Howells qtd. in Bentley, 2.

15. Thomas Johnson in his 1955 edition gave Dickinson's most productive year as 1862; Franklin's more recent dating assigns 227 poems to 1862 and an astonishing 295 to 1863 (*Poems* 1533). Under either editor's dating, the coincidence between Dickinson's peak poetic activity and the crisis of the Civil War is striking.

16. "'A house divided against itself cannot stand.' I believe this government cannot endure, permanently half *slave* and half *free*. I do not expect the Union to be *dissolved* – I do not expect the house to *fall* – but I *do* expect it will cease to be divided." Abraham Lincoln, "House Divided" (delivered June 16, 1858), in Roy P. Basler, ed., *Lincoln: Speeches and Writings 1832–1858* (New York: Library of America, 1989), 426.

17. On the launch of conscription and its reach towards Austin Dickinson, see Faith Barrett, "Dickinson's War Poems in Discursive Context," in Martha Nell Smith and Mary Loeffelholz, eds., *A Companion to Emily Dickinson* (Malden and Oxford: Blackwell Publishing, 2008), 118–19.

18. Barrett, "Dickinson's War Poems," 118.

19. On Austin Dickinson's payment of a substitute, see Barrett, "Dickinson's War Poems," 119.

20. See Ed Folsom's online commentary and photographs, "Whitman, Dickinson & Mathew Brady's Photos." www.classroomelectric.org/volume2/folsom/brady.html, and Renée Bergland, "The Eagle's Eye: Dickinson's View of Battle," in Smith and Loeffelholz, eds., *A Companion to Emily Dickinson*, 145–47.

21. Folsom, "Whitman, Dickinson & Mathew Brady's Photos," n.p.

22. Eliza Richards, "'Death's Surprise, Stamped Visible'": Emily Dickinson, Oliver Wendell Holmes, and Civil War Photography," *Amerikastudien / American Studies* 54.1 (2009), 13–33, 28.

23. Eliza Richards, "'How News Must Feel When Traveling': Dickinson and Civil War Media," in Smith and Loeffelholz, eds., *A Companion to Dickinson*, 164.

24. The Metropolitan Museum of Art's superb 2013 exhibition on "The Civil War and American Art" juxtaposed Frederic Church's painting and other paintings and photographs of the American Civil War with the poetry of Dickinson and Whitman; see the catalog of the exhibition by Eleanor Jones Harvey, *The Civil War and American Art* (Washington, DC and New Haven, CT: The Smithsonian Art Museum and Yale University Press, 2013) on Dickinson's wartime

aesthetic, shared with Church and other painters, of "destabilized weather and portents in the skies" (43).

25. Richards, "'Death's Surprise,'" 28.

26. Bergland, "'The Eagle's Eye,'" 153.

27. Habegger, *My Wars Are Laid Away in Books*, 402–03.

28. Wilfred Owen, "Dulce Decorum Est" (1920), in Edmund Blunden, ed., *The Collected Poems of Wilfred Owen* (New York: New Directions, 1965), 55; Marianne Moore, "In Distrust of Merits," *Complete Poems* (1967; New York: Macmillan/Viking, 1981), 137. On the contrast between World War I's "protest literature of combatants" such as Owen and "the new readiness of women, a generation later, to talk back to them" in women's World War II poetry, see Susan Schweik, *A Gulf So Deeply Cut: American Women Poets and the Second World War* (Madison and London: The University of Wisconsin Press, 1991), 5–6; Schweik sees Moore's poem as "a response to her distance from the violence of which she is attempting to make sense" (42).

29. Bergland, "'The Eagle's Eye,'" 154.

30. Benedict Anderson, *Imagined Communities: Reflections on the Origin and Spread of Nationalism* (1983; rev. edn. London and New York: Verso, 1991), 6, 145.

31. Anderson, *Imagined Communities*, 145.

32. Masako Takeda, "Dickinson in Japan," in Domhnall Mitchell and Maria Stuart, eds., *The International Reception of Emily Dickinson* (London and New York: Continuum, 2009), 173.

33. Christopher E. G. Benfey, "A Route of Evanescence: Emily Dickinson in Japan," *The Emily Dickinson Journal* 16.2 (2007), 81.

34. On the Kyoto conference program, see the *Emily Dickinson International Society Bulletin* 19.2 (November/December 2007), available at www.emilydickinsoninternationalsociety.org/sites/defa ult/files/EDIS%20NovDec2007.pdf.

35. Naoki Onishi, "Emily Dickinson Knew How to Suffer," *Emily Dickinson International Society Bulletin* 23.2 (November/ December 2011), 4–5.

5 FAITH AND DOUBT

1. Allen Tate, *Reactionary Essays on Poetry and Ideas* (New York: Charles Scribner's Sons, 1936), 13.

2. Tate, *Reactionary Essays*, 14; Vendler, *Poems and Commentaries*, 226, 230.

3. Vendler, *Poems and Commentaries*, 38. This poem circulated widely in various versions during Dickinson's lifetime, including publication in print in the *Springfield Daily Republican* (March 1, 1862) as well as several different versions sent to Susan Gilbert Dickinson and another to Thomas Wentworth Higginson. Vendler's discussion explores the poetic value of each distinct version.

4. Vendler, *Poems and Commentaries*, 42.

5. Lord's health had been precarious for many years; he suffered a stroke on March 11, 1884 and died at home March 1. See Jay Leyda, *The Years and Hours of Emily Dickinson*, 2 vols. (New Haven: Yale University Press, 1960), II: 418–19.

6. James McIntosh, *Nimble Believing: Dickinson and the Unknown* (Ann Arbor: the University of Michigan Press, 2000), 1; Elisa New, "Difficult Writing, Difficult God: Emily Dickinson's Poems beyond Circumference," *Religion & Literature* 18.3 (Fall 1986), 4.

7. McIntosh, *Nimble Believing*, 1.

8. Vendler, *Poems and Commentaries*, 495.

9. Samuel Taylor Coleridge, *Biographia Literaria* (1817; New York: George P. Putnam, 1848), II: 442.

10. Jonathan Edwards, "The Most High a Prayer-hearing God" (1736), in *Practical Sermons, Never Before Published* (Edinburgh: M. Gray, 1788), 68–69.

11. Deppmann, *Trying to Think With Emily Dickinson*, 15.

12. On Dickinson's personal counterparts to public worship, see W. Clark Gilpin, *Religion Around Dickinson* (University Park: The Pennsylvania State University Press, 2014), 96–97.

13. Psalm 121 is the only text in Dickinson's Bible on which a marginal inscription survives. Her friend Eliza Coleman left a brief note of her visit to Dickinson during Amherst College's commencement week in the summer of 1854 – "E.M.C. 14th Aug[t] 1854" – accompanied by a pressed flower. *The Holy Bible, containing the Old and New Testaments: translated out of the original tongues* (Philadelphia: J. B. Lippincott & Co., 1853; Dickinson Family Library copy, EDR 8, Houghton Library, Harvard University, Cambridge, MA), 564–65.

14. Gilpin, *Religion Around Emily Dickinson*, 176.

15. Vendler, *Poems and Commentaries*, 510, 508.

16. Vendler, *Poems and Commentaries*, 393–94.

17. Vendler, *Poems and Commentaries*, 205, 207.

18. *The Poetical Works of George Herbert* (New York: D. Appleton, 1857; Dickinson Family Library copy, EDR 63, Houghton Library, Harvard University, Cambridge, MA), 241; the Houghton curators believe that marks of use in this copy inscribed as Susan Dickinson's indicate Emily Dickinson's reading. Dickinson certainly knew something of Herbert; she copied out two stanzas of his "Mattens," probably from its appearance in the *Springfield Daily Republican* for October 28, 1876, which were later attributed in error to Dickinson herself (Franklin, *Poems* III: 1583).

6 THE SPIRIT LASTS – BUT IN WHAT MODE –

1. For a presentation of the entire manuscript and its visual line breaks as continuous rather than a note followed by stanzas, see Hart's "The Encoding of Homoerotic Desire," 251–52.
2. Miller, *Reading in Time*, 10, 12.
3. Walter J. Ong, *Orality and Literacy: The Technologizing of the Word* (London: Methuen, 1982), 136.
4. Gilpin, *Religion Around Emily Dickinson*, 64.
5. Socarides, *Dickinson Unbound*; Cotter, "A Poet who Pushed (and Recycled) the Envelope."
6. Franklin, *Poems*, III: 1353. For an extended and influential critique of Franklin's editing of this manuscript as exemplary of Dickinson's posthumous conscription into "lyric reading," see Jackson, *Dickinson's Misery*, 22–38. It seems to me, however, as it does to Eliza Richards, that "Dickinson herself received and arguably worked within" the generic template of the lyric, before it became a condition of her posthumous reception. See Richards's review of *Dickinson's Misery* in *The New England Quarterly* 80.3 (Fall 2007), 511.
7. Franklin, *Poems*, I: 163. Perhaps remarkably, these lines seem to be the only such transcription apparently made from memory of a Dickinson poem that turned up between Johnson's edition and Franklin's; they were first published by David J. M. Higgins in "Twenty-five Poems by Emily Dickinson: Unpublished Variant Versions," *American Literature* 38.1 (March 1966), 21.
8. Ong, *Orality and Literacy*, 128.
9. William Ellery Channing, *Self-Culture: An Address Introductory to the Franklin Lectures, Delivered at Boston, September, 1838* (Boston: Dutton and Wentworth, 1838), 42–43; see also Gilpin, *Religion Around Emily Dickinson*, 70–73.

10. Given this poem's subject, it bears repeating that the line breaks of interest to me in this reading are those that can be heard as well as seen, where the end of the manuscript's visual line coincides with the division between lines as measured out by syllables in the poem's regular aural pattern, rather than the purely visual breaks occasioned when Dickinson ran out of space on the manuscript page.

11. Edward Hitchcock, *Religious Lectures on Peculiar Phenomena in the Four Seasons* (Amherst: J. S. and C. Adams, 1850), 10, 17.

12. Noah Webster, *An American Dictionary of the English Language*, 2 vols. (Amherst: J. S. and C. Adams, 1844), II:145a.

13. Claude Shannon, "A Mathematical Theory of Communication" (1948), cited in James Gleick, *The Information: A History, A Theory, A Flood* (2011; New York: Vintage Books, 2012), 3.

14. Dickinson also used versions of the four lines beginning "The Rumor's Gate was shut so tight" in a number of other manuscripts from 1883, including several beginning with the line "This me that walks and works must die"; see Fr 1616.

15. Visitors to the Emily Dickinson Archive who click "read more" on the home page will find a very brief essay surveying Dickinson's writing practices, the discovery and editing of the mass of her manuscript writings after her death, and acknowledging that "Since those first editorial transcriptions, there has been debate about the importance of the manuscript page to our understanding of Dickinson's poetry" (www.edickinson.org/, n.p., accessed February 19, 2015) – debate so intense that it very nearly prevented the Advisory Board from arriving at any consensus statement acknowledging that debate's existence. An FAQ page (www.edickinson.org/faq) helps readers unfamiliar with the manuscripts or with editorial scholarship place what they may see in looking at the manuscript pages, including marks that are not Dickinson's own. For a brief account of the public launch of the Emily Dickinson Archive, how the Dickinson family's War between the Houses became and remained the tussle between the colleges of Harvard and Amherst, and the differences among the scholars who contributed to it, see Jennifer Schuessler, "Enigmatic Dickinson Revealed Online," *New York Times*, October 23, 2013, C1.

16. For images of the new daguerreotype and discussions of the efforts made thus far to authenticate it, see the web page "A New Dickinson Daguerreotype?" maintained by the Jones Library of Amherst College at www.amherst.edu/library/archives/holdings/edickinson/new_da guerreotype, and the Dickinson Electronic Archive's exhibition and forum at www.emilydickinson.org/1859daguerreotype.

17. Richard B. Sewall's *The Life of Emily Dickinson* (1974; New York: Farrar, Straus and Giroux, 1980), reproduces a photograph owned by Herman Abromson and inscribed on the reverse "Emily Dickinson 1860," conceding that "Opinions vary as to whether it is an authentic picture of Emily Dickinson, the poet" (752). Forensic investigation later determined that the inscription was a forgery. Albert Habegger's *My Wars Are Laid Away in Books* reproduces the photograph bought by Philip Gura on eBay in 2000 (photo insert, between 366 and 367) and makes an elaborate case for its authenticity, speculating along with Gura that the image may be a copy from the late 1880s of a daguerreotype originally sent to Charles Wadsworth in 1855, in Appendix 1 (634–37). On the forensic investigation of the Abromson portrait, the doubtful provenance of the Gura photograph, and the "substantial differences in the facial images" (13) of the Gura photograph next to the authentic daguerreotype, see George Gleason, "Is It Really Emily Dickinson?" *The Emily Dickinson Journal* 18.2 (2009), 1–20.

18. www.amherst.edu/library/archives/holdings/edickinson/new_daguer reotype, n.p., accessed February 17, 2015.

19. "About the Archive," Dickinson Electronic Archives, http://archive.e milydickinson.org/about_the_site.html, n.p., accessed February 17, 2015. In "Networking Dickinson: Some Thought Experiments in Digital Humanities," *The Emily Dickinson Journal* 23.1 (Spring 2014), 106–19, I assess some digital Dickinson projects focused on non-lexical properties of her manuscripts and suggest some alternative approaches.

20. Cotter, "A Poet who Pushed (and Recycled) the Envelope."

21. Leslie A. Morris, "Happy Birthday, Emily Dickinson Archive!" October 23, 2014; http://blogs.law.harvard.edu/houghtonmodern/ 2014/10/23/happy-birthday-emily-dickinson-archive/. Accessed June 16, 2015. It must be conceded that the Harvard-based archive is biased towards lexical content in its search mechanisms and other aspects of presentation; by contrast, the online Dickinson collections of Amherst College put the visual appearances of the manuscripts up front. In-depth comparisons of how visitors use the two sites will present an extraordinary research opportunity.

22. See Miller, *Reading in Time*; Deppman, *Trying to Think with Emily Dickinson*, especially chapter 4, "Amherst's Other Lexicographer" (109–49); and Michelle Kohler, *Miles of Stare*, chapter 4: "Scarce Opon

My Eyes: Fleeting Visions and the Epistemology of Metaphor in Dickinson's Poetry" (105–36).

23. See http://shelleygodwinarchive.org/.

24. Jackson, *Dickinson's Misery*, 1.

25. See Lyndall Gordon, *Lives Like Loaded Guns: Emily Dickinson and Her Family's Feuds* (New York: Viking, 2010), 252–53.

Bibliography

Unless otherwise noted, Dickinson's poems and letters are quoted from and cited by the numbers assigned them in the following editions:

Franklin, R. W., ed. *The Poems of Emily Dickinson: Variorum Edition.* 3 vols. Cambridge, MA: The Belknap Press of Harvard University Press, 1998.

Johnson, Thomas H., and Theodora Ward, eds. *The Letters of Emily Dickinson.* 3 vols. Cambridge, MA: The Belknap Press of Harvard University Press, 1958.

WORKS CITED

Anderson, Benedict. *Imagined Communities: Reflections on the Origin and Spread of Nationalism.* 1983. Rev. edn. London and New York: Verso, 1991.

Austen, Jane. *Persuasion.* 1818. Cambridge and New York: Cambridge University Press, 2006.

Axelrod, Stephen. *Sylvia Plath: The Wound and the Cure of Words.* Baltimore and London: The Johns Hopkins University Press, 1990.

Barrett, Faith. "Dickinson's War Poems in Discursive Context." In Martha Nell Smith and Mary Loeffelholz, eds., *A Companion to Emily Dickinson.* Malden and Oxford: Blackwell Publishing, 2008, 107–32.

Basler, Roy P., ed. *Lincoln: Speeches and Writings 1832–1858.* New York: Library of America, 1989.

Benfey, Christopher E. G. "A Route of Evanescence: Emily Dickinson in Japan." *The Emily Dickinson Journal* 16.2 (2007): 81–93.

Bennett, Paula Bernat. "'Looking at Death, Is Dying': Fascicle 16 in a Civil War Context." In Paul Crumbley and Eleanor Elson Heginbotham, eds., *Dickinson's Fascicles: A Spectrum of Possibilities.* Columbus: Ohio State University Press, 2014, 106–29.

"The Pea that Duty Locks: Lesbian and Feminist-Heterosexual Readings of Emily Dickinson's Poetry." In Karla Jay and Joanne Glasgow, eds., *Lesbian Texts and*

Contexts: Radical Revisions. New York: New York University Press, 1990, 104–25.

Bentley, Nancy. *Frantic Panoramas: American Literature and Mass Culture 1870–1920*. Philadelphia: University of Pennsylvania Press, 2009.

Bergland, Renée. "The Eagle's Eye: Dickinson's View of Battle." In Martha Nell Smith and Mary Loeffelholz, eds., *A Companion to Emily Dickinson*. Malden and Oxford: Blackwell Publishing, 2008, 133–56.

Bervin, Jen, and Marta Werner, eds. *The Gorgeous Nothings: Emily Dickinson's Envelope-Poems*. New York: Christine Burgin/New Directions, 2013.

Bingham, Millicent Todd. *Emily Dickinson: A Revelation*. New York: Harper & Brothers, 1954.

Blunden, Edmund, ed. *The Collected Poems of Wilfred Owen*. New York: New Directions, 1965.

Browning, Elizabeth Barrett. *Prometheus Bound, and Other Poems*. New York: C. S. Francis; Boston: J. H. Francis, 1851. EDR 525, Houghton Library of Harvard University, Cambridge, MA.

Bushell, Sally. "Meaning in Dickinson's Manuscripts: Intending the Unintentional." *Emily Dickinson Journal* 14.1 (2005): 24–61.

Cameron, Sharon. *Choosing Not Choosing: Dickinson's Fascicles*. Chicago: University of Chicago Press, 1992.

Channing, William Ellery. *Self-Culture: An Address Introductory to the Franklin Lectures, Delivered at Boston, September, 1838*. Boston: Dutton and Wentworth, 1838.

Coleridge, Samuel Taylor. *Biographia Literaria*. New York: George P. Putnam, 1848.

Cotter, Holland. "A Poet Who Pushed (and Recycled) the Envelope" (rev. of Jen Bervin and Marta Werner, eds., *The Gorgeous Nothings*). "Books of the Times," *New York Times*, December 6, 2013, C32.

Crumbley, Paul. *Winds of Will: Dickinson and the Sovereignty of Democratic Thought*. Birmingham: University of Alabama Press, 2010.

Davidson, Michael. "Introduction: Women Writing Disability." *Legacy: A Journal of American Women Writers* 30.1 (January 2013): 1–17.

Deppman, Jed. *Trying to Think with Emily Dickinson*. Amherst: University of Massachusetts Press, 2008.

Dillon, Elizabeth Maddock. *The Gender of Freedom: Fictions of Liberalism and the Literary Public Sphere*. Stanford: Stanford University Press, 2004.

Doane, Mary Anne. "Film and Masquerade." *Screen* 23.3–4 (September–October 1982): 74–87.

"Masquerade Reconsidered: Further Thoughts on the Female Spectator." *Discourse* 11.1 (Fall–Winter 1988–1989): 42–54.

Edwards, Jonathan. *Practical Sermons, Never Before Published*. Edinburgh: M. Gray, 1788.

Emerson, Ralph Waldo. *Essays: Second Series*. Boston: James Munroe & Co., 1844.

Emily Dickinson Archive. www.hup.harvard.edu/features/dickinson/. Cambridge, MA: Harvard University Press. Accessed July 5, 2013.

Emily Dickinson Historic Vinyl Wall Graphic Decal Sticker. www.amazon.com/WGH58082-Dickinson-Historic-Graphic-Historical/dp/B008L0NKUS/ref=pd_sim_sbs_misc_6. Accessed June 25, 2013.

Erkkila, Betsy. "Dickinson and the Art of Politics." In Vivian Pollak, ed., *A Historical Guide to Emily Dickinson*. New York: Oxford University Press, 2004. 133–74.

The Wicked Sisters: Women Poets, Literary History, and Discord. New York and Oxford: Oxford University Press, 1992.

Farr, Judith. *The Passion of Emily Dickinson*. Cambridge, MA and London: Harvard University Press, 1992.

Folsom, Ed. "Whitman, Dickinson & Mathew Brady's Photos." www.classroomelectric.org/volume2/folsom/brady.html. Accessed January 7, 2015.

Franklin, R. W., ed. *The Manuscript Books of Emily Dickinson*. Cambridge, MA: The Belknap Press of Harvard University Press, 1981.

Freedman, Linda. *Emily Dickinson and the Religious Imagination*. Cambridge and New York: Cambridge University Press, 2011.

Gelpi, Albert J. *The Tenth Muse: The Psyche of the American Poet*. Cambridge and New York: Cambridge University Press, 1991.

Gilbert, Sandra, and Susan Gubar. *The Madwoman in the Attic: The Woman Writer and the Nineteenth-Century Literary Imagination*. New Haven: Yale University Press, 1979.

Gilpin, W. Clark. *Religion Around Emily Dickinson*. University Park: The Pennsylvania State University Press, 2014.

Gleason, George. "Is It Really Emily Dickinson?" *The Emily Dickinson Journal* 18.2 (2009): 1–20.

Gordon, Lyndall. *Lives Like Loaded Guns: Emily Dickinson and Her Family's Feuds*. New York: Viking, 2010.

Gray, Erik. *The Poetry of Indifference: From the Romantics to the Rubaiyat*. Amherst: University of Massachusetts Press, 2005.

Green, Laura. *Literary Identification from Charlotte Brontë to Tsitsi Dangarembga*. Columbus: The Ohio State University Press, 2012.

Guillory, John. *Cultural Capital: The Problem of Literary Canon Formation.* Chicago: University of Chicago Press, 1993.

Habegger, Alfred. *My Wars Are Laid Away in Books: The Life of Emily Dickinson.* New York: Random House, 2001.

Halperin, David and Valerie Traub, eds. *Gay Shame.* Chicago: University of Chicago Press, 2010.

Haltunnen, Karen. *Confidence Men and Painted Women: A Study of Middle-Class Culture in America, 1830–1870.* New Haven: Yale University Press, 1982.

Hart, Ellen Louse. "The Encoding of Homoerotic Desire: Emily Dickinson's Letters and Poems to Susan Dickinson, 1850–1886." *Tulsa Studies in Women's Literature* 9.2 (Autumn 1990): 251–72.

and Martha Nell Smith. *Open Me Carefully: Emily Dickinson's Intimate Letters to Susan Huntington Dickinson.* Ashfield: Paris Press, 1998.

Heaney, Seamus. *Death of a Naturalist.* 1966. Repr. London: Faber & Faber, 1988.

Herbert, George. *The Poetical Works of George Herbert.* New York: D. Appleton, 1857.

Hewitt, Elizabeth. *Correspondence and American Literature, 1770–1865.* Cambridge, MA: Cambridge University Press, 2004.

Higgins, David J. M. "Twenty-five Poems by Emily Dickinson: Unpublished Variant Versions." *American Literature* 38.1 (March 1966): 1–21.

[Higginson, Thomas Wentworth.] "Ought Women to Learn the Alphabet?" *The Atlantic Monthly* 3. 16 (February 1859): 137–50.

and Mabel Loomis Todd, eds., *Poems by Emily Dickinson.* Boston: Roberts Brothers, 1890.

and Mabel Loomis Todd, eds., *Poems by Emily Dickinson* (Second Series). Boston: Roberts Brothers, 1891.

Hitchcock, Edward. *Religious Lectures on Peculiar Phenomena in the Four Seasons.* Amherst: J. S. and C. Adams, 1850.

Howe, Susan. *My Emily Dickinson.* Berkeley: North Atlantic Books, 1985.

The Birth-mark: Unsettling the Wilderness in American Literary History. Middletown: Wesleyan University Press, 1993.

Jackson, Virginia. *Dickinson's Misery: A Theory of Lyric Reading.* Princeton: Princeton University Press, 2005.

Juhasz, Suzanne, and Cristanne Miller. "Comic Power: A Performance." *The Emily Dickinson Journal* 5.2 (Fall 1996): 85–92.

Kohler, Michelle. *Miles of Stare: Transcendentalism and the Problem of Literary Vision in Nineteenth-Century America.* Tuscaloosa: University of Alabama Press, 2014.

Leyda, Jay. *The Years and Hours of Emily Dickinson*, 2 vols. New Haven: Yale University Press, 1960.

Lipking, Lawrence. *The Life of the Poet: Beginning and Ending Poetic Careers.* Chicago: University of Chicago Press, 1981.

Loeffelholz, Mary. "Corollas of Autumn: Reading Franklin's Dickinson." *The Emily Dickinson Journal* 8.2 (Fall 1999): 55–71.

   Dickinson and the Boundaries of Feminist Theory. Urbana and Chicago: University of Illinois Press, 1991.

   "Networking Dickinson: Some Thought Experiments in Digital Humanities." *The Emily Dickinson Journal* 23.1 (Spring 2014): 106–19.

McIntosh, James. *Nimble Believing: Dickinson and the Unknown.* Ann Arbor: University of Michigan Press, 2000.

Merrill, James. "The Book of Ephraim." In *Divine Comedies: Poems.* New York: Atheneum, 1980, 47–136.

Miller, Cristanne. *Reading in Time: Emily Dickinson in the Nineteenth Century.* Amherst: University of Massachusetts Press, 2012.

Mitchell, Domhnall. *Measures of Possibility: Emily Dickinson's Manuscripts.* Amherst and Boston: University of Massachusetts Press, 2005.

Mitchell, Domhnall, and Maria Stuart, eds. *The International Reception of Emily Dickinson.* London: Continuum, 2009.

Moon, Michael, ed. *Leaves of Grass and Other Poems by Walt Whitman.* New York: W. W. Norton, 2002.

Moore, Marianne. *Complete Poems.* 1967. New York: Macmillan/Viking, 1981.

Morris, Leslie A. "Happy Birthday, Emily Dickinson Archive!" October 23, 2014; http://blogs.law.harvard.edu/houghtonmodern/2014/10/23/happy-birthday-emily-dickinson-archive/. Accessed June 16, 2015.

Murray, Aife. *Maid as Muse: How Servants Changed Emily Dickinson's Life and Language.* Hanover: University Press of New England, 2010.

Nagy, Gregory. *The Ancient Greek Hero in 24 Hours.* Cambridge, MA: The Belknap Press of Harvard University Press, 2013.

New, Elisa. "Difficult Writing, Difficult God: Emily Dickinson's Poems beyond Circumference." *Religion & Literature* 18.3 (Fall 1986): 1–27.

Ong, Walter J. *Orality and Literacy: The Technologizing of the Word.* London: Methuen, 1982.

Onishi, Naoki. "Emily Dickinson Knew How to Suffer." *Emily Dickinson International Society Bulletin* 23.2 (November/December 2011): 4–5.

Patterson, Rebecca. *The Riddle of Emily Dickinson.* Boston: Houghton Mifflin, 1951.

Phillips, Elizabeth. *Emily Dickinson: Personae and Performance*. University Park: Pennsylvania State University Press, 1988.

Plath, Sylvia. *Ariel*. New York: Harper & Row, 1965.

 The Colossus and Other Poems. 1960, 1962. Repr. New York: Vintage/Random House, 1998.

 Letters Home: Correspondence 1959–1963. Ed. Aurelia Schober Plath. London: Faber & Faber, 1975.

 The Unabridged Journals of Sylvia Plath. Ed. Karen V. Kukil. New York: Vintage Books, 2007.

Porter, David. *Dickinson: The Modern Idiom*. Cambridge, MA: Harvard University Press, 1981.

Prins, Yopie. "'Lady's Greek' (With the Accents): A Metrical Translation of Euripides by A. Mary F. Robinson." *Victorian Literature and Culture* 34 (2006): 591–618.

Reynolds, David S. *Beneath the American Renaissance: The Subversive Imagination in the Age of Emerson and Melville*. Cambridge, MA and London: Harvard University Press, 1988.

Rich, Adrienne. "Vesuvius at Home: The Power of Emily Dickinson." 1975. Repr. *On Lies, Secrets and Silence: Selected Prose 1966–1978*. New York: W. W. Norton, 1979.

Richards, Eliza. " 'Death's Surprise, Stamped Visible: Emily Dickinson, Oliver Wendell Holmes, and Civil War Photography." *Amerikastudien / American Studies* 54.1 (2009): 13–33.

 "'How News Must Feel When Traveling': Dickinson and Civil War Media." In Martha Nell Smith and Mary Loeffelholz, eds., *A Companion to Dickinson*. Malden and Oxford: Blackwell Publishing, 2008, 157–79.

 Review of *Emily Dickinson's Shakespeare* by Paraic Finnerty and *Dickinson's Misery: A Theory of Lyric Reading* by Virginia Jackson. *New England Quarterly* 80.3 (Fall 2007): 507–12.

Rosenthal, M. L. and Sally Gall. *The Modern Poetic Sequence: The Genius of Modern Poetry*. New York: Oxford University Press, 1983.

Runzo, Sandra. "Dickinson, Performance, and the Homoerotic Lyric." *American Literature* 68.2 (June 1996): 347–63.

Said, Edward. *On Late Style: Music and Literature Against the Grain*. New York: Pantheon Books, 2006.

Salska, Agnieszka. *Walt Whitman and Emily Dickinson: Poetry of the Central Consciousness*. Philadelphia: University of Pennsylvania Press, 1985.

Schuessler, Jennifer. "Enigmatic Dickinson Revealed Online." *New York Times*, October 23, 2013, C1.

Schweik, Susan. *A Gulf So Deeply Cut: American Women Poets and the Second World War*. Madison and London: The University of Wisconsin Press, 1991.

Sedgwick, Eve Kosofsky. *Epistemology of the Closet*. Berkeley and Los Angeles: University of California Press, 1990.

Sewall, Richard B. *The Life of Emily Dickinson*. 1974. New York: Farrar, Straus and Giroux, 1980.

Shannon, Claude. "A Mathematical Theory of Communication," cited in James Gleick, *The Information: A History, A Theory, A Flood*. New York: Vintage Books, 2012.

Shurr, William. *The Marriage of Emily Dickinson: A Study of the Fascicles*. Lexington: University Press of Kentucky, 1983.

Smith, Martha Nell. *Rowing in Eden: Rereading Emily Dickinson*. Austin: University of Texas Press, 1992.

and Mary Loeffelholz, eds. *A Companion to Emily Dickinson*. Malden and Oxford: Blackwell Publishing, 2008.

Socarides, Alexandra. *Dickinson Unbound: Paper, Process, Poetics*. New York: Oxford University Press, 2012.

Stewart, Susan. "On ED's 754/764." *New Literary History* 45.2 (Spring 2014): 253–70.

Taggard, Geneviève. *The Life and Mind of Emily Dickinson*. New York: A. A. Knopf, 1930.

Takeda, Masako. "Dickinson in Japan." In Domhnall Mitchell and Maria Stuart, eds., *The International Reception of Emily Dickinson*. London and New York: Continuum, 2009, 173–88.

Tate, Allen. *Reactionary Essays on Poetry and Ideas*. New York: Charles Scribner's Sons, 1936.

Todd, Mabel Loomis, ed. *Poems by Emily Dickinson*. Third Series. Boston: Roberts Brothers, 1896.

Trilling, Lionel. *The Experience of Literature*. New York: Holt, Rinehart and Winston, 1967.

Van Dyne, Susan R. *Revising Life: Sylvia Plath's Ariel Poems*. Chapel Hill and London: University of North Carolina Press, 1993.

Vendler, Helen. *Coming of Age as a Poet: Milton, Keats, Eliot, Plath*. Cambridge, MA: Harvard University Press, 2003.

Dickinson: Selected Poems and Commentaries. Cambridge, MA: Harvard University Press, 2010.

Poets Thinking: Pope, Whitman, Dickinson, Yeats. Cambridge, MA: Harvard University Press, 2004.

Walsh, John Evangelist. *The Hidden Life of Emily Dickinson*. New York: Simon and Schuster, 1971.

Webster, Noah. *An American Dictionary of the English Language*. 2 vols. Amherst: J. S. and C. Adams, 1844.

Weisbuch, Robert. *Emily Dickinson's Poetry*. Chicago: University of Chicago Press, 1975.

Werner, Marta L. *Radical Scatters: Emily Dickinson's Late Fragments and Related Texts, 1870–1886*. http://jetson.unl.edu:8080/cocoon/radicalscatters/default-login.html. Accessed July 9, 2013.

Ravished Slates: Revisioning the "Lord" Letters. www.emilydickinson.org/ravished-slates-re-visioning-the-lord-letters. Accessed February 1, 2015.

Whitmarsh, Tim. *Narrative and Identity in the Ancient Greek Novel: Returning Romance*. Cambridge, MA: Cambridge University Press, 2011.

Index

Amherst College, 1, 20, 51, 122, 126, 130, 131, 132, 141n12, 146n13, 148n15, 149n21
Anderson, Benedict, 96–7
Arnold, Matthew, 57
Austen, Jane, *Persuasion*, 78, 143n2
Axelrod, Stephen, 142n29

Barrett Browning, Elizabeth, 62, 73; *Aurora Leigh*, 71–2, 141n24; *Sonnets from the Portuguese*, 38, 138n1
Benfey, Christopher, 97
Bennett, Paula Bernat, 39, 135n5
Bergland, Renée, 95, 96
Bible, The, 105–6, 125; *I Corinthians*, 29; *Exodus* 20, 46; *Exodus* 33, 111; *Genesis* 1, 104; *Genesis* 29, 51; *John* 15, 113; *John* 19, 40; *Mark* 10, 46, 107; *Matthew* 22, 71; *Matthew* 26, 126; *Psalm* 121, 111, 146n13
Bingham, Millicent Todd, 40
blasphemy, 29, 44, 105, 110
Bowles, Samuel, 96, 139n16
Bradstreet, Anne, 82; *Brontë, Charlotte*, 1, 51, 59; *Jane Eyre*, 71–2, 141n24
Brontë, Emily, 141n24
Browning, Robert, 69
Bushell, Sally, 137n18

Cameron, Sharon, 4, 26, 32
Channing, William Ellery, 124
Church, Frederic, 95, 144n24
Civil War, The American, 5, 9, 16, 18, 83, 91–6, 144n15; photography in, 94–6
Clark, Charles H., 128
Coleridge, Samuel Taylor, 107
Coleman, Eliza, 146n13
Columbia University, 57, 73
common meter, 12, 125
Communion sacrament, 112–17
Copeland, Aaron, 99
Cooper, James Fenimore, 69

Cotter, Holland, 20, 36, 120, 133
Crumbley, Paul, 84, 86, 143n7

Davidson, Michael, 138n13
Deppmann, Jed, 108–9, 133, 136n13
Dickinson, Austin, 36, 52, 91, 93, 128, 130
Dickinson, Edward, 31, 41; *political career of*, 83
Dickinson, Edward ("Ned"), 52, 105, 106, 109
Dickinson, Emily, and Christianity, 28–29, 31, 40, 44–6, 56, 86, 103–17; *and classical Greek literature*, 45–6, 53–4, 61–2, 84, 134; *daguerreotypes of*, 1, 8, 131–2, 148n16, 149n17; *in digital reproduction*, 7–8, 129–34; *editing of*, 2–4, 6–7, 99–101, 134; *eye troubles of*, 18, 55, 136n11; *fascicles of*, 4–6, 16, 17–18, 23–4, 118, 137n21; *fragments of*, 5, 130; *and the gaze*, 79–82, 84, 87, 90; *handwriting of*, 2, 6, 12–15, 18, 118–19, 134; *Japanese reception of*, 97–8; *and labor*, 18, 86, 89; *letters of*, 5–6, 37, 118; *and lyric poetry*, 5, 147n6; *and marriage*, 47–53; *and "Master,"* 38, 50, 51, 53, 62, 139n16; *material media*, 9–10, 20, 118–21, 129, 132; *and memory*, 55–6, 118–20, 122–3, 129–34; *and publication*, 6, 28, 34; *and shame*, 50–53; *variants*, 4, 23, 32, 118; *and writing technologies*, 134
editions: *Poems* (*1890*), 2, 37, 47, 80, 99–101; *Poems, Second Series* (*1891*), 2, 21, 130; *Poems, Third Series* (*1896*), 2; *Bolts of Melody* (*1945*), 57; *The Poems of Emily Dickinson* (*1955*), 3, 57, 144n15; *The Poems of Emily Dickinson* (*1998*), 3, 4, 10, 99, 144n15, 147n6
letters
  Letters 93, 44
  Letters 119, 23

Dickinson, Emily, and Christianity (cont.)
 Letters 121, 23
 Letters 151, 23
 Letters 166, 52
 Letters 173, 51
 Letters 187, 38
 Letters 233, 38, 50, 53
 Letters 234, 72
 Letters 248, 38, 50
 Letters 256, 27
 Letters 261, 47
 Letters 280, 91
 Letters 559, 40–41
 Letters 575, 42, 49
 Letters 671, 126
 Letters 750, 63, 64
 Letters 751, 63, 141n12
 Letters 752, 141n12
 Letters 804, 128
 Letters 811, 71
 Letters 855, 114
 Letters 871, 128
 Letters 912, 55
 Letters 968, 104
 Letters 1036, 104
 poems
  "A brief, but patient illness – " (Fr 22), 29
  "A Coffin – is a small Domain" (Fr 890), 103
  "A sepal – petal – and a thorn" (Fr 25), 29
  "A single Screw of Flesh" (Fr 293), 46, 54
  "A Word made Flesh is seldom" (Fr 1715), 113
  "Adrift! A little boat adrift!" (Fr 6), 24–6, 29, 32
  "'And with what Body do they come'?" (Fr 1537), 126–7
  "As if I asked a common alms – " (Fr 14), 26–7
  "As the Starved Maelstrom laps the Navies" (Fr 1064), 114, 117
  "Because I could not stop for Death – " (Fr 479), 99–101, 133
  "By such and such an offering" (Fr 47), 24
  "Dare you see a Soul at the White Heat" (Fr 401)
  "Did the Harebell loose her girdle" (Fr 134), 74
  "Essential Oils are wrung – " (Fr 772), 35

"Garlands for Queens, may be – " (Fr 10), 28–9
"'Go tell it' – What a Message – " (Fr 1584), 57–62, 64, 66
"God made a little Gentian – " (Fr 520), 33–4, 111
"He ate and drank the precious Words – " (Fr 1593), 113
"'Heavenly Father' – take to thee" (Fr 1500), 109–10
"I cannot live with you" (Fr 706), 4, 37, 45, 53
"I got so I could hear his name – " (Fr 292), 45–6, 81–2
"I had a guinea golden – " (Fr 12), 26–7
"I had been hungry, all the Years – " (Fr 439), 115–17
"I heard a Fly buzz – when I died – " (Fr 591), 101–02, 104, 125
"I heard, as if I had no Ear" (Fr 996), 125–7
"I never lost as much but twice – "" (Fr 39), 29, 31
"I prayed, at first, a little Girl" (Fr 546), 112
"If 'God is Love' as he admits" (Fr 1314), 103
"If I may have it, when it's dead" (Fr 431), 45, 49
"I'm ceded – I've stopped being theirs " (Fr 353), 37, 47, 49
"I'm Nobody! Who are you!" (Fr 260), 75
"I'm Wife – I've finished that – " (Fr 225), 37
"In the name of the Bee – " (Fr 23), 29
"I should have been too glad, I, see – " (Fr 283), 45
"It always felt to me – a wrong" (Fr 521), 105
"It feels a shame to be Alive – " (Fr 524), 92–3, 94–5
"I've known a Heaven, like a Tent – " (Fr 257), 79–82, 84, 87, 88, 90
"Like Trains of Cars on Tracks of Plush" (Fr 1213), 74
"Mine – by the Right of the White Election" (Fr 411), 4, 37, 47–9
"My Life had stood – a Loaded Gun – " (Fr 764), 67–72, 133, 142n32

"My period had come for Prayer – " (Fr 525), 110–12

"My Portion is Defeat – today – " (Fr 704), 93–5

"No Brigadier throughout the year" (Fr 1596), 106

"No Crowd that has occurred" (Fr 653), 129

"Nobody knows this little Rose" (Fr 11), 27–8

"Of all the Souls that stand create – " (Fr 279), 40, 44, 45, 53, 55, 70–71

"Of all the Sounds despatched abroad" (Fr 334), 47

"Of God we ask one favor, that we may be forgiven – " (Fr 1675), 109, 116

"Oh what a Grace is this – " (Fr 1669), 105

"On this wondrous sea" (Fr 3), 23, 24–6

"Power is a familiar growth" (Fr 1287), 17

"Prayer is the little implement" (Fr 623), 108–9

"Rearrange a 'Wife's' Affection!" (Fr 267), 49–54, 66, 138n11

"Safe in their alabaster chambers" (Fr 124), 34, 102–3, 122–3, 146n3

"She slept beneath a tree – " (Fr 15), 30

"Show me eternity, and I will show you Memory – "" (Fr 1658), 55–6, 119–20

"So has a Daisy vanished" (Fr 19), 29

"Some keep the Sabbath going to Church – " (Fr 236), 110

"Strong Draughts of Their Refreshing Minds" (Fr 770), 113

"Struck was I nor yet by lightning" (Fr 841), 38

"The Bible is an antique Volume – " (Fr 1577), 105–7

"The Brain – is wider than the Sky – " (Fr 598), 8–10, 123

"The Fact that Earth is Heaven – " (Fr 1435), 105

"The Gentian has a parched Corolla – " (Fr 1458), 18, 34–6

"The Gentian weaves her fringes" (Fr 21), 27, 29–30

"The Grass so little has to do – " (Fr 379), 80–81

"The incidents of Love" (Fr 1172), 54

"The Mind lives on the Heart" (Fr 1384), 64

"The Mushroom is the Elf of Plants" (Fr 1350), 19–23, 35, 73–5, 137n18

"The name – of it – is 'Autumn' – " (Fr 465), 95

"The Props assist the House –" (Fr 729), 85–8, 95

"The Robin's my Criterion for Tune – " (Fr 256), 77–9, 80, 84, 96–7

"The smouldering embers blush – " (Fr 1143), 53–4, 62

"The Spirit is the Conscious Ear – " (Fr 718), 123–5, 126

"The Spirit lasts – but in what mode – " (Fr 1627), 127–9

"There came a day – At Summers full – " (Fr 325), 2, 37, 42–45, 47, 113, 130

"These are the days when Birds come back – " (Fr 122), 113

"'They have not chosen me' – he said – " (Fr 87), 112–13

"Though the great Waters sleep" (Fr 1641), 104

"Through the strait pass of suffering" (Fr 187), 111

"Title divine – is mine!" (Fr 194), 45

"To lose – if One can find again – " (Fr 30), 30–32

"'Twas a long parting, but the time" (Fr 691), 37

"'Twas just this time, last year, I died" (Fr 344), 102–3

"'Twas warm – at first – like Us – " (Fr 614), 102

"Unto a broken heart" (Fr 1745), 98

"We pray – to Heaven – " (Fr 476), 108

"When Roses cease to bloom, Sir" (Fr 8), 13–17, 21, 27

"When what they sung for is undone" (Fr 1545), 120–22, 147n6

"Where Roses would not dare to go" (Fr 1610), 13–17, 21

"While it is alive" (Fr 287), 37–8

"Whole Gulfs – of Red, and Fleets – of Red – " (Fr 468), 95

"Wild Nights – Wild Nights!" (Fr 269), 4, 32

"Your thoughts dont have words every day" (Fr 1476), 113

"You've seen Balloons set – Hav'nt You!" (Fr 730), 85, 87–90
Dickinson Electronic Archives, 130–32
Dickinson, Gilbert, 128
Dickinson, Lavinia ("Vinnie"), 36, 134
Dickinson, Susan Huntington Gilbert, 18, 23, 25, 34, 42, 44, 51–2, 54–6, 87, 106, 114, 118, 119, 128, 134, 139n16, 146n3
Dillon, Elizabeth Maddock, 138n12
Doane, Mary Ann, 140n7

Edwards, Jonathan, 69, 82, 106; "The Most High a Prayer-Hearing God," 108, 110, 111–12
Eliot, George, 12, 62
Eliot, T. S., 5, 12; "The Waste Land," 57
Emerson, Ralph Waldo, 62, 63, 82, 83; "Experience," 86–7; "The Poet," 77, 79, 80
Emily Dickinson Archive, The, 7–8, 21, 130–34, 148n15, 149n21
Emily Dickinson International Society, The, 97–8
Emmons, Henry Vaughn, 23, 51, 52
Erkkila, Betsy, 72, 141n24, 143n6, 143n7

Farr, Judith, 139n16
feminist literary criticism, 59–60, 65–72, 82–3, 140n7, 141n24
Folsom, Ed, 94
Franklin, Ralph W., The Manuscript Books of Emily Dickinson, 137n21; The Poems of Emily Dickinson, 3, 4, 6, 10, 15, 18, 23–4, 28, 51, 91, 99, 120, 122, 130, 147n6
Freedman, Linda, 45, 53
Frost, Robert, 80
Frye, Northrop, 39–40, 44

Gelpi, Albert, 82
Gilpin, W. Clark, 113
Gleason, George, 149n17
Gordon, Lyndall, 41
Gray, Erik, 18
Green, Laura Morgan, 51, 52
Guillory, John, 140n4
Gura, Philip, 131, 149n17
Gutenberg Project, The, 1, 3

Habbeger, Alfred, 12, 19, 53, 139n17, 149n17
Halperin, David, 50
Haltunnen, Karen, 90
Hart, Ellen Louise, 55, 139n20, 147n1
Harvey, Eleanor Jones, 144n24
Hawthorne, Nathaniel, 72, 82; The Scarlet Letter, 48
Heaney, Seamus, "Digging," 30–1
Herbert, George, 147n18; "Love (III)," 116
Hewitt, Elizabeth, 87
Higgins. David J. M., 147n7
Higginson, Thomas Wentworth, 2, 3, 7, 21, 23, 27, 34, 37, 42, 47, 80, 101, 110, 118, 146n3; in the Civil War, 91; "Letter to a Young Contributor," 27; "Ought Women to Learn the Alphabet?" 64, 72
Hitchcock, Edward, 126–7
Homer, 59; Iliad, 61
homoeroticism, 61, 131
Hopkins, Gerard Manley, 3
Houghton Library of Harvard University, 7, 130, 148n15
Howe, Julia Ward, 91–2, 93
Howe, Susan, 3–4, 73; My Emily Dickinson, 67–70, 141n20
Howells, William Dean, 90

information, 127, 129

Jackson, Helen Hunt, 109
Johnson, Thomas H., 3, 57, 120; The Letters of Emily Dickinson, 10, 141n12
Jackson, Virginia W., 5–6, 7, 8, 133, 141n22, 147n6
Joyce, James, 1, 12

Keats, John, 90; Hyperion and Fall of Hyperion, 45; "Ode to a Nightingale," 57
Kimball, Benjamin, 104
Kohler, Michelle, 81, 133

Lincoln, Abraham, 91, 95, 144n15
Lipking, Lawrence, 11
Lord, Otis Phillips, 40–42, 62–4, 104, 139n16, 141n12, 146n5

Marvell, Andrew, 57
McIntosh, James, 105, 106

Melville, Herman, 83; *Battle-Pieces*, 91; *Moby-Dick*, 82
Merchant, Natalie, 99
Merrill, James, 39–40, 44
Miller, Cristanne, 89; *Reading in Time*, 17–18, 120, 124, 133
Milton, John, 1, 71; "Lycidas," 57
Mitchell, Domhnall, 137n18
Moore, Marianne, 58; "In Distrust of Merits," 96, 145n28
Morris, Leslie, 149n21
Moses, 105, 111
Mount Holyoke Seminary, 105
Murray, Aïfe, 136n11

Nagy, Gregory, 61
nationalism, 77, 96–7
New, Elisa, 105
Newton, Benjamin, 63
Norcross, Louise and Frances, 21, 23, 72

Ong, Walter J., 120, 121, 124
Onishi, Naoki, 98
orality, 120, 123–4
Owen, Wilfred, 96, 145n28

Patterson, Rebecca, 131
Phillips, Elizabeth, 48
Plath, Sylvia, 5, 73–6; "Ariel," 75–6, 142n31, 142n32; bee poems, 74; "Mushrooms," 73–5
Porter, David, 12
prayer, 108–12
Prins, Yopie, 61
Prometheus, 45–6, 53–4, 62

resurrection, 40, 126–7, 129
Reynolds, David, 83
Rich, Adrienne, 73; "Vesuvius at Home," 66–9, 141n20
Richards, Eliza, 94, 95, 147n6
Root, Abiah, 51–2
Rosenthal, M. L., and Sally M. Gall, 5
Runzo, Sandra, 138n13, 140n7

Said, Edward, 11
Salska, Agnieszka, 82
Sappho, 59, 73, 118
Schuessler, Jennifer, 148n15

Schweik, Susan, 145n28
Sedgwick, Eve Kosofsky, 51, 53
Sewell, Richard, 131, 149n17
Shakespeare, William, 1, 66, 69; *King Lear*, 57, 69; Sonnet 130 ("My mistress' eyes are nothing like the sun"), 65, 66; *The Tempest*, 75
Shannon, Claude, 127
Shelley, Percy Bysshe, 133; "Ode to the West Wind," 57; *Prometheus Unbound*, 45; "With a Guitar, to Jane," 75
Shelley-Godwin Archive, 133
Shurr, William, 38, 138n12
Simonides, epitaph for the Spartans, 58–59, 60, 64
slavery, 68, 83, 91
Smith, Martha Nell, 55, 130, 131; *Rowing in Eden*, 6, 139n16
Smith College, 73, 74
Socarides, Alexandra, 120, 138n26
Sophocles, 59; *Oedipus Rex*, 57
spiritual autobiography, 86
Springfield Daily Republican, The, 23, 28, 34, 62, 146n3, 147n18
Stewart, Susan, 142n32

Taggard, Geneviève, 141n24
Takeda, Masako, 97
Tate, Allen, 99, 101
Tennyson, Alfred, "Ulysses," 61
Thoreau, Henry David, *Walden*, 27, 82
Todd, Mabel Loomis, 2, 3, 7, 12, 13, 21, 37, 40, 57, 60, 101, 122, 129, 130, 134, 138n11
Traub, Valerie, 50
Trilling, Lionel, 57–60, 63
Turner, Katherine Scott Anthon, 131–2
Twain, Mark, 1, 107

Van Dyne, Susan, 75, 142n31
Vendler, Helen, *Coming of Age as a Poet*, 11, 23, 74; *Dickinson: Selected Poems and Commentaries*, 29, 44, 79, 86, 101, 102, 103, 113, 114, 115; *Poets Thinking*, 54, 137n19

Wadsworth, Charles, 52, 62, 63, 128, 139n16, 139n17, 149n17
Walsh, John Evangelist, 141n24

Werner, Marta, 5, 20, 41, 42
Weisbuch, Robert, 5
Whitman, Walt, 5, 82; *Drum-Taps*, 91; *Leaves of Grass* (1855), 85, 89
Whitmarsh, Tim, 61

Woolf, Virginia, 1, 59
Wordsworth, William, 78

Yeats, William Butler, 5; "The Circus Animals' Desertion," 22, 137n19

Printed in the United States
By Bookmasters